EXPERT OR CHARLATAN?
The Rise and Rise of Management Consulting

Dr. **John Louth** B.Sc. (ECON) M.Sc. Ph.D. ACMA CGMA

KNOWLEDGE WORLD

KW Publishers Pvt Ltd
New Delhi

2011 FPBA BEST PUBLISHERS AWARD (ENGLISH)

KNOWLEDGE WORLD

KW Publishers Pvt Ltd

4676/21, First Floor, Ansari Road, Daryaganj, New Delhi 110002

Email: knowledgeworld@vsnl.net Tel.: +91.11.23263498/43528107

www.kwpub.com

ISBN 978-93-83649-06-8

Published by Kalpana Shukla, KW Publishers Pvt Ltd

4676/21, First Floor, Ansari Road, Daryaganj, New Delhi 110002

Printed and bound in India

Contents

Foreword

Around the time I was asked to write this foreword I went to a dinner party and ended up chatting to a friend's daughter—young, smart, sassy and just out of Oxbridge. I asked her what she wanted to do with her life and she told me that she wanted to get a well-paid senior job for 15 years and then do something worthwhile—so she had decided to initially become a management consultant. I groaned (inwardly) then read this book and realised that she fits the picture perfectly.

Or does she? I have known John Louth for twelve years—a period that spans him being a senior officer in the Royal Air Force, to management consultancy, to his current persona as an academic, think tank professional and specialist adviser to politicians. During that period I have, formally, been his teacher, supervisor of his doctoral work, co-author of academic papers and now mentor. But formalities belie a more generative and mutual relationship and friendship, where we have challenged each others' thoughts and ideas, and shared insights from very different worlds. *Is this what management consultancy is?* I find myself asking, somewhat nervous of having my stereotypes fractured. Probably not, I conclude, having read this book.

The world is a dangerous place for all kinds of unrecognised reasons. Change, audit, performance management, accountability, risk analyses, profit and growth are concepts that can easily generate psychosis as our grasp of reality slips away into a world where failure, loss of status, economic collapse and rejection figure large. The size, speed, range and complexity of work tasks can overwhelm and promote real anxiety—for both the professional inside organisations and the informed citizen.

As this book makes clear, into this world comes management consulting, with its therapeutic and redeeming capabilities. Management consulting offers answers and solutions to those troublesome troubles and worrying worries. Absent here is any nuanced understanding or knowing. Rather, it authoritatively deploys a range of standardised (and therefore, it is assumed, reliable and robust) technologies of management to any given situation. The manager can be assured that, if everyone else is using it, it must be good. PowerPoint presentations convey the clarion call. And the high priests of the technology, the purveyors of the PowerPoint, are comforting. The comfort of the management consultant comes from the price tag, the cut of their suits, their facility with the technology of management and the ability to make a sale.

Management consulting might therefore be seen, benignly, as an empty ritual—a fulfilment of the needs of managers to assuage their fears and justify their actions. And, if it makes everyone feel better, where is the harm? Does it matter if your consultant is John Louth or my young companion at the dinner party?

I think it does matter. In his professional practice and in this book John combines a rare acuity for what happens in and between organisations with an ability to analyse and understand without the occlusion generated by the standardised management technologies that so many are prepared to buy. Such originality of insight steps clearly away from the management consultancy model, and may make it unsustainable in its current form.

This book poses the challenge that management consultants should be possessed of intelligence, expertise, reflexivity, original thinking, substantial experience and, above all, a critical nature. They should be the wary, best friends of managers—the jesters at the court of senior management, with licence to criticise, challenge and make fools of their paymasters. But in the vignettes described in this book, such a management consultant, dressed in motley and not a sharp suit, might well be unlikely to be tolerated or even hired in the first place.

The consequences of the absence of such critical, challenging consultants are, as this book makes clear, potentially very dangerous indeed. We run the very real risk of group-thinking leading us up the veritable garden path to "success" that is entirely self-referential and authorised by management consultants hired by those seeking to demonstrate their superb capabilities. If this book is right, or even partially right, and the many Emperors of Management Consultancy have no clothes, then this needs to be shouted from every rooftop and this book is a valuable first step in that direction.

Rebecca Boden

Introduction
The Prince and the Admiral—How Did I Get Here?

An Audience at the Palace

The day palace of the royal family of a wealthy Middle East emirate is a cross between a place of government and a ludicrously ornate family home where brothers (the men are, of course, dominant in this part of the world) meet to consider family and state business—the two things are interchangeable in their minds. It is undoubtedly over-air conditioned inside, but then it is unbelievably hot outside, though the gardens with their excessive and continuous watering and feeding seem immune to the heat. I wasn't though: I was sweating going into the palace and now the cold beads of my perspiration were being dried by the forced air of an expensive Middle Eastern air conditioning system so that, perversely, I was shivering in the middle of the desert. I was dressed, like my colleagues, in a Western business suit but surrounded by a number of rich-looking young, well-groomed, swarthy gentlemen in full Arabian dress as we moved into our third hour of PowerPoint briefings to a clearly bored young prince.

This was what I did. The Emirate's royal family, through one of their wealth funds and corporations, paid the company I worked for a modest fortune to advise the Emirate on the development of a particular economic free zone. I led this work, doing a bit of research, talking across the world to a large group of disparate companies who might conceivably be interested in opportunities in the Middle East and, thereafter, putting together a programme and plan to bring the free zone alive. Every three months or so I had to brief the sponsoring prince on progress, travelling to the day palace to "show and tell" western genius by relaying to him, slide by slide, a teasing PowerPoint presentation. By the hundredth slide he was inwardly screaming in submission, though on the outside the picture of sophisticated, intelligent enquiry, and it was easy to get his agreement that all milestones had been met and the programme was performing to time and costs. I even made up some Key Performance Indicators which proved an enormous thrill to his advisory team.

My principal colleague was a huge American called Ian. He had commanded an aircraft carrier in the US Navy and was clearly not a huge fan of anybody suffering under the misfortune of either not being born an American or having the honour to serve in the armed forces of the land of the free and the home of the triple-burger. His role was to look Western, tall and powerful (in contrast, I come across as short and geeky), not to speak too much and to give the young prince the assurance that an American retired admiral was on his side. Ian sat quietly brooding with a senior officer look on his face feigning sincerity and intelligence, neither of which, in truth, was a natural state for this battle-weary American.

At the end of the briefing and the customary add-on hour of small talk the prince led his delegation of advisers away towards the Royal Mosque on the ground floor of the palace for afternoon prayers. Having been speaking for the best part of three and a half hours I was desperate to get out of there and to find the soft comfort of my hotel's bar. The problem was I had misplaced Ian; an unlikely occurrence given that he was over six and a half feet tall and easily weighed two hundred and fifty pounds. Also a potentially dangerous happening as the palace was swarming with armed guards who had a reputation for dealing with the uncertain by shooting rather than questioning. "Where could the mad fool be?" formed in my mind at the same time as I heard voices raised in alarm, even anger, from the unlikely direction of the Prince's entourage. From what I could hear it was clear that Ian had meekly followed the prince assuming he was being escorted politely to the palace door before realising with the horror of a born-again US Christian that he was heading straight for *the* royal mosque.

No way was a gung-ho son of America entering a mosque and there was little chance the Emirate's royals were going to allow this gum-chewing non-believer anywhere near their most cherished family place of worship. We were stuck in the worst of all places in the Middle East: a social embarrassment involving race, religion and business. Maybe to save face the Arabs would just kill him.

I told myself that we had, probably already, escaped death hours earlier when arriving at the Palace. As we were exiting our cars, marshalled by both soldiers and close protection officers, a fast-travelling shiny Porsche had torn into the car park and executed a questionable high-speed stop not far from our gaggle of Westerners. The pristine pink gravel of the palace's parking area was sent in all directions, travelling at the speed of bullets, and I followed the example of my Arab minders and ducked to avoid a face-full of stone chippings. One of our guards launched himself at full-speed towards the car and I feared, for a moment, that I was about to be at the centre of come terrorist outrage. Not to worry; the guard was merely tearing-off after the Porsche's keys that had been thrown casually into the air from a younger prince as he exited his car. The guard knew his interests were best served by catching the keys before they hit the ground, which he duly did, exercising a cat-like leap and forward roll onto the hard and sharp gravel. I'd like to think the young prince was pleased by this act of devotion, but it was impossible to tell. I could only see his disappearing back as he entered the palace, oblivious to the commotion he had caused. Ian had the last word before we entered to commence our lengthy briefing.

"Well, Toto, we're not in Kansas now."

As is the habit of retired senior military officers the world over, Ian's insights had the knack of being simultaneously correct and utterly useless but, I suppose, that is how greatness is made. For myself, I needed to think for a moment or two to understand just where I was and how on earth I arrived here, the supposed consulting expert, about to break bread with my prince.

I worked for a company based in London which specialised in products and services for the defence and security sectors. My job was to lead complex consulting engagements, usually for the British Ministry of Defence, but also for any client anywhere in the world happy to pay my employer's fees. My day rate was usually around $ 2,000.00 plus expenses, and I had found myself almost by accident heading-up a small multidisciplinary team from different advisory companies working on a programme for the leaders of this Emirate.

This programme's proposition was both simple and surreal. A national company from the Emirate called Zala, owned by the royal family and chaired by my princely overseer, would develop a massive business park exclusively for the world's defence and security companies. The royal family would make as much land available as was necessary for the success of the venture—the figure of 225 square kilometres was frequently bandied about—

with the business park intended to be located just to the northeast of the existing passenger airport for the Emirate. Zala's wish was to construct a dedicated marine port and dockyard to service the business area, as well as its own exclusive runway. To top it off, the whole area would be classed as a special economic zone enabling companies from around the world to undertake operations free from the burdens of tax or awkward employee rights. My role was to develop the overall concept, suggest the right mix of businesses to make it a viable self-sustaining proposition and to oversee the development of the master plan and investment models.

Not surprisingly, many of the world's leading companies had expressed an interest in the development with a few of the larger advisory businesses forming part of my little planning consortium. This meant that a number of quite different personalities were working together for the first time, which was proving quite a challenge. As well as Ian I was working closely with Nigel, a partner from the world's largest business advisory group. Nigel was only interested in the money and, more importantly, the proportion of it that would flow into his hands. Whilst supremely professional and cafe-au-lait smooth, Nigel did not warm to the concept or the client and thought Ian a fool and an indulgence. Ian thought Nigel an insincere, plastic "Brit"—goodness knows what they both thought of me—and between the three of us we formed the leadership of the defence free zone project, working for the prince and his managing director, a remarkable man called Engineer Jalleb.

Jalleb was a sincere and considerate Emirati who loved his country and was dedicated and loyal to his chairman and prince. He was generous, thoughtful and an engaging host and, I am sure, a most able engineer. He was not, most certainly, a good businessman nor an effective controller of consultants. Jalleb's most pressing concern, which took almost all of his attention, was to oversee and test the PowerPoint pack that was used to brief the prince. I spent hours with Jalleb and his Board going through slide after slide to demonstrate what had been done or was to be done. This was before they would allow me anywhere near their prince. If Jalleb had read a book on performance management, I would make up one or two indicators to demonstrate that performance would be managed. His finance director liked the technique out of America that thought activities could be managed as a "balanced scorecard"—I developed a slide that discussed the free zone's Development Balanced Scorecard, and so on, so that governance of the project became the PowerPoint pack itself and a number of disparate but fashionable themes therein. Nigel cut and paste into the pack a financial model from a previous project which gave the client confidence that we understood the deep financial issues driving the project and that we were the men to manage the risks and exploit the obvious opportunities. It felt more like a marketing exercise or sales pitch than the activities of the leadership of a project to deliver major economic benefits. And this went on, in this fashion, for almost eighteen months.

Vignette of My Consulting Life

The point to make is that this was far from unusual. Rather, in many ways, this brief vignette of my time in the Emirate is the classic descriptor of life as a management consultant. A needy client, clever consultants, travel, complex proposals boiled down to simplicities, huge sums of money and the overall whiff of deals to be done, would be themes recognised by anybody either working in the advisory sphere or employing consultants. Indeed, the sense of need from the client, and the consultant's ability to meet that need, is at the core of the relationship. The gentle concern, I suppose, is the manner in which the consultant helps to inform, construct and articulate the need, if the answer is more or less always the skills—PowerPoint slides?—offered by the consultant.

As a consequence of my time in the emirate and elsewhere I set myself two questions. *How* does the concept of management consultancy work and *why* does it work? This short book is the product of the search for the answers.

In organising my responses to these two interrelated questions I have sought to give my readers both a practitioner's subjective impression of management consultancy and some hard conceptual analysis and ideas from which to draw. In Section 1, therefore, I talk a little about the consulting profession and what consultants actually do, compared against the profound uncertainty in the geopolitical system and world economy. I hint at why the global consulting business in the twenty-first century finds the worlds of the Middle East, Africa and Asia/Pacific rim so attractive and ripe for the expansion of business.

I then go on in Section 2 to discuss my role as expert, assessing the range of products, techniques and practices that, together, comprise the tool kit of the successful consultant. Common themes are unpacked such as those associated with transformation and change; portfolio, programme and project management and recovery; economic analyses and strategy, and risk and opportunity management and planning. These management areas and other subjects are all conceptualised and framed by the consultant's ever-present skill in business development and sales, so that consulting solutions and delivery are *operationalised* through whatever the practitioner can sell. Though, inevitably, the dominant narrative is of the expert generating significant economic, programmatic or organisational benefits and outcomes for his or her clients.

Section 3 talks a little about the psychology of consulting, its powerful legitimising narrative, and the dependency culture between client and practitioners. Thereafter, the conclusion, at Section 4, discusses the possibility of a reform agenda for consultancy within the international political and economic system. I am clear though that this journey is most certainly subjective, it is far from exhaustive and it leaves some stones unturned. But it is sincere, where possible evidence-based, and offered without cynicism. It is, after all, a slice of my life, derived from my own history and experience, presented as both apology and aria.

What it is not, most definitely, is a complete history of the practices of management consulting so far. Books like that are available, and one or two have informed this work as the footnotes will reveal. I am not a historian and felt that a new economic and practitioner history of the subject was best left to somebody else. Also, as a defence and security analyst, inevitably I frame my world in reference to defence and security themes. Many of my examples, therefore, are drawn from this environment. This is natural, and sensible, within a piece derived from personal experience and reflection.

My contention, moreover, is that the world is a complicated and uncertain place with many hazards and risks; a place often best understood in part through the lens of international stability and national security. Management consultancy does not always take account of this complexity. In expanding upon this point in the text I drift into a geopolitical analysis and the challenges facing states and their peoples. Given my academic background and past engagement with the military, I hope the reader allows me this conceit and even considers it to be a strength of the work.

SECTION ONE

1. A Confident Proposal—The Globalisation of Management Consultancy

An Omnipotent Expertise

A consultant, of course, is a universal term for describing a person who provides a service, or offers a set of future benefits, to another. In the context of management consultancy, that service is usually for a fee in exchange for some skill or competency that is, somehow, not possessed by the client. The consultant is imbued with a sense of expertise, prestige, experience and knowledge which is highly valued, and valuable, in the marketplace where the consultant and his or her clients reside. It is this sense of expertise and rare knowledge that gives the profession its allure and power. The core proposition, if you like, is the idea that the consultant knows more than the client and should be rewarded for imparting that precious knowledge.

Traditionally, the management consultant's area of expertise is, as the name suggests, in the arena of organisation and business, whether for profit or within some kind of public or social sector. The consultant therefore conducts his profession through the practice of the diagnosis of business or organisational problems, failures or potential weaknesses and the framing of potential solutions often deployed through the lexicon of change management, which I shall come to shortly. The key point is that this practice is perceived as professional, useful, repeatable, codifiable and capable of being successful—that is, in exercising the deliberate changes thought necessary to generate organisational success. It makes for a powerful legitimising narrative for the employment of management consultants. Significantly, it permeates global businesses and government activities alike, not discriminating between the two sectors.

When I worked as a consultant, the underlying message to potential clients was that I could diagnose the problems he or she felt existed within the business, programme or project and that I could both manage the implementation of my solution and, by extension, manage the entity much better than the established senior management team. So this idea of "management" is also important to the definition.

Notions of Management

Management is a generic, all-embracing term, which I have always found difficult to quantify and define.[1] Child[2] describes management as an elite grouping, transforming policy into outcomes, whilst Drucker[3] believes that it can be summarised as a function, as well as the people discharging it; a discipline rather than a hierarchical social grouping. Management, therefore, is best captured through an intellectual perspective or school of thought rather than a prescriptive definition.

Taylor's[4] work on "scientific management" has dominated the Classical School. He believed that the role of management was to rationalise and master processes through which human actions could be normalised, measured and controlled leading to significant increases in business efficiency. Indeed, he argued there was a causal link between effective management and organisational efficiency. Taylor provided guiding principles on the division of labour and standardisation which dominated the industrial landscape through their application, for example, in

Henry Ford's motor factories in the USA. Fayol[5] contributed to the Classical School by distinguishing between management activity and other organisational behaviour, focusing on planning, organisation, coordination, command and control.

Developing from the Classical School, Simon[6] focused on the ability of managers to make good decisions in conditions of uncertainty; a forerunner to today's management of risk. This Decision Theory School, in contrast to classical theory, argues that the process of decision-making is neither rational nor scientific. Sub-optimising factors can and do occur to blunt management action.

Drucker argues that the approach should be functional—that is, to assess what managers actually do rather than what they should be doing. This is mirrored, in many ways, in the work of Mintzberg[7] and Kotter[8] who contributed towards the functional tradition by identifying the key activities of management, through an analysis of the tasks practitioners were performing. These could be summarised under the headings of agenda setting, communicating and networking.

Stewart[9] in contrast, argues that situational factors significantly impact upon the behaviour of individual managers. The components of the model he develops—demands, choices and constraints—define the nature of the work undertaken and drive the managerial approach. The response to earlier theories and approaches to management is to regard it as a subjective, personal activity.

In summarising these theorists and schools it is easy to assert that management is a complicated concept, which can be assessed in a number of contradictory ways. Management consultancy, of course, as a practice does not articulate its approach to the theory of management and is not aligned to a specific school or theory.

Rather, the discipline of management consultancy champions the concept of management itself. The point here, of course, is that it is this sense of management as rational discourse through all its functions and forms that is important to both consultant and client, with this discourse a bounded commodity that can be traded and sold.

Big Business

In 2000, the global revenues for management consultancy businesses were in excess of $ 114 billion. By 2005, that had risen to $ 200 billion per annum peaking in 2008 at approximately $ 250 billion. Despite a huge global financial crisis originating in the sub-prime mortgage market in the United States, in 2012 those annual revenues were still holding-up above the $ 200 billion level, with clients and governments in the developing world and growth economies such as India and China replacing revenues streams lost to consultancies from clients in North America and Europe.[10] These are huge numbers by anybody's standards, which we should just reflect upon for a moment. For example, a country like the Philippines has a population in excess of ninety-three million people, with a gross domestic product of $ 188 billion, less than the total annual revenues of the management consulting profession. And this is a country that is growing at six per cent per annum and seen as a magnet for Asian expansion and opportunity.[11] Understanding how management consultancy enjoys such impressive returns internationally, and hegemony over the international economy, becomes an important set of organisational and governmental questions. But, for me, it is also a profound sociological puzzle seeking a response.

It is, perhaps, simpler to understand where the industry has come from. Based on the earlier definition, management consultants can be conceptualised as anybody who helps another with a business or organisational problem in a time-bound fashion, probably for a fee or some other consideration or benefit. On this definition, consultants have most probably been around since the dawn of time. Any professional who used their skill or time to help a fellow could be seen as an early consultant. So a blacksmith in pre-industrial England helping a fellow in the adjacent village to establish and develop his own smithy was a consultant as, perhaps, was the village elder in sub-Sahara Africa considering water usage for the community. Yet, somehow, the very notion of a professional management consultant and the industry the term gives rise to only makes sense in a modern context as a consequence of the industrial revolution.

During the late eighteenth and early nineteenth centuries as industrialisation swept Europe and North America, consultants with business, organisational, production and factory experience and acumen helped to design, develop and implement ideas around business organisation, the lay-out of production lines, the specialisation and division of labour and so on. Consequently a number of firms were born from about 1850 onwards that specialised in these business and organisational practices. They were typically derived from members of the accounting and engineering professions who had worked in business and wanted to promote their ideas across wider aspects of the economy or across society as a whole.

For example, in the early twentieth century James O. McKinsey left his job as a public accountant to found McKinsey & Co. to provide strategy, financial and management advice to senior corporate leaders in businesses in the United States. These same skills were seen to be needed by the US federal government with McKinsey's reputation as a global strategy house born as a consequence of the fusion between business and governmental practices and experiences.

The twentieth century, especially in the period following the Great War of 1914 to 1918, saw an explosion in the demand for consultancy services by businesses and government departments and, as in any free market economy where demand outstrips supply, new entrants were enticed into a booming market. This was especially significant as the start-up costs for new consultancies were perceived as minimal. It was very simple: if consultants could sell services successfully, and repeat those sales, the consultant would be successful independent of long-term client results. Moreover, those successful advisory businesses in parallel industries such as accountancy saw the successes enjoyed in the management consultancy world and coveted those, relatively, easy and durable income streams. Consequently, in the twentieth century the recognised large national and international accounting firms such as Andersen, Price Waterhouse, Coopers and Lybrand, Deloitte and Touche, Ernst & Young and KPMG, amongst others, developed and opened their own consultancy practices to supplement their financial reporting, audit and management accounting activities. Given these practices' deep and long-standing accounting and reporting relationships with the largest corporations on the planet, these large accounting firms would come to dominate the consulting market so that by the end of the twentieth century, when the informed lay person thought of management consultancy, they thought intuitively of PricewaterhouseCoopers (PwC), KPMG and Deloitte as well as the traditional strategy houses such as McKinsey.

At the turn of the twenty-first century the world's largest international accountancy partnerships were amongst the top ten global management consultancies and accounted for almost half of all revenues generated by the top fifty consultancy firms from around the world.[12] It is very big business indeed, and there is little doubt that the global accountancy firms have imbued the practice of consultancy with global credibility and the lure of a professional cadence, so that:

These firms have become aggressive marketers in the consulting industry to attract clients from all walks of life, purchasing prime time television and radio advertising slots as well as entire sections of newspapers and magazines. It even seems that these firms have purchased every illuminated poster of billboard space in airports, plastering their names all over walls and kiosks to target business travellers who may one day hire a consultant.[13]

These businesses and the practice of consultancy itself has been able to thrive and develop to an unprecedented scale despite complexity, geopolitical uncertainty and across international trade because the consultant, in part, has been able to tap into this uncertainty as a core element of her or his pitch to potential clients. Consequently if uncertainty, risks and change are not core corporate competencies they become the preserve of the consultant who uses them as tradable commodities to promote the advisory business.

Deconstructing complexity, diagnosing uncertainty and risks, and the management of change have become the key components of the consulting profession so that, paradoxically, the immense systemic complexities that we come on to discuss in this volume feed the consulting profession, with the latter reinforcing the sense of complexity and uncertainty within the international system. Put simply, there is good business in chaos, complexity and collapse. The consultant today may not properly understand the variables of the client's interaction with the broader parts of the economy, but fuelling uncertainty and dependency is enough to generate opportunities in a sales-led approach to consultancy, as perfected historically by the large accountancy practices drawn to consultancy.

Why Consultants are in Demand

There are a number of straightforward reasons why the consultancy market has developed to generate the sorts of huge annual revenues we discussed earlier and why consultants appear perennially in demand. First, a curious, fortunate and profitable, feature of the industry is that the management consultant is perceived to be needed right through the economic cycle, from boom and growth through to recession and fiscal constraint. For instance, during economically challenging times consultants are said to be required for their cost-cutting skills or their reorganising and protective strategy advice. Whilst, in contrast, during the good times consultants help firms and governments develop their growth plans and match organisational competencies to emerging market trends and business opportunities. It is a neat trick of the consultant to always be needed irrespective of the operating environment or broader geopolitical and economic conditions.

Second, and as already touched upon, the barriers to entry into the profession are minimal as intellectual capital and the ability to make a sale to a potential client are the only real requirements. In short, anybody can set themselves up as a management consultant—indeed, this is often one of the principal criticisms made against the industry. Moreover, the operating model of most consultancies help to keep costs low as business expenses such as travel, subsistence and even the employment of specialist subcontractors are all billed back to the client. With the dexterous use of agreed invoicing and payment schedules the financial risks to which the consultant could be exposed can really be kept to a minimum. It is a most attractive way of working for both those of sharp brain and sharp practice.

The Life of a Consultant

There is, of course, no cloned management consultant defining the market but there are common attributes that frame the life of the typical management consultant. These merit discussion for they can help identify more broadly the practices of consulting itself. However, it is important to note straightaway that the life of the consultant is intrinsically wedded to the operating style and structure of the consulting business he or she operates within. My simple contention is that there are some readily identifiable features and factors defining both—the consultant and the business of management consultancy.

Most consultancy businesses describe themselves as meritocracies and professional, collegiate places to work where management layers are kept to a minimum. A quick glance at the website of any consultancy will find aspirations and assertions like these in positions of prominence on the web pages being reviewed. Yet, in reality, management consultancy practices—especially the international brands—are generally highly bureaucratic, hierarchical and competitive places to dwell.[14] Though naturally different in terms of size, the number of offices and perhaps even the work performed, management consulting firms seem to have particularly uniformed structures. At the bottom of the pile, holding up all the others, are the support staff and administrators. Above these in the pecking order are the research analysts, the "worker bees" of the outfit, and the level at which most aspiring consultants join the business, usually straight from university or a business school. The consultants or senior consultants are more seasoned professionals who have cut their teeth as analysts earlier in their careers. These members of the firm usually have some management responsibilities, perhaps supervising or mentoring analysts, and invariably have sales targets. The principal consultants come next, the people who typically lead engagements on a day-to-day basis, and who hold project or relationship management responsibilities. At the apex of the firm, however, sit the partners or directors. They typically have an equity stake in the business and have senior responsibilities for client management, business development and the forward strategy of the firm and its overall governance. These men and women have usually taken a number of years lumbering, or in some cases flying, through the preceding levels of the business and are very protective of the consulting brand and their individual firm's reputation. What is striking, however, is just how stratified and bureaucratic the typical consulting firm appears to be, especially at a time when information technology and the communications revolution has driven flatter, less hierarchical organisations to the fore. Indeed, many consultants would sell the latter as the ideal organisational solution to which clients should aspire.

Within the multilayered consulting business different competencies and attributes are demanded from practitioners at different stages of their careers. As fledgling consultants, analysts are expected to undertake repeat research, analytical and data mining activities. Through this they often generate a good understanding of a particular market or industry which, in turn, allows them to be promoted to more client-facing roles within a specific business or for a particular engagement. At the top of the firm the partners generate new business, contribute to brand recognition and awareness and engage in market management through speaking engagements, the generation of papers and articles and widespread networking with potential clients and broader industry and governmental groups. These specific roles and responsibilities, aligned as they are to status and appointment, have hardly shifted from the inception of consulting as an organised profession, say in the 1850s, to the present day.

Given the hierarchical nature of the typical consulting firm and the notional activities at each level of the business, just what is it that management consultants actually do with their time? To help answer this question let us turn to the work of Ethan M. Rasiel. He joined the consultants McKinsey & Co. in 1989 in the United States undertaking a number of consulting engagements on behalf of the firm, especially with client companies in the finance, telecommunications, information technology and consumer goods sectors. He has subsequently written a number of books about his time with McKinsey & Co. which illuminate the activities of a typical consultant.[15]

There are two things initially to note from Rasiel's writings. The first is the almost spiritual manner with which he discusses McKinsey. For those who are unaware, McKinsey & Co. is still probably one of the leading global strategy advisory businesses, influencing the activities of governments and corporations alike. When the British government in the late twentieth century wished to transform its defence procurement arm in a multi-billion dollar change programme with profound significance to Britain's capacity for defence and force projection, it turned to McKinsey for strategic advice and to design the programme the government would subsequently get others to roll-out. Incidentally, an independent report commented on this change programme that the Ministry of Defence:

> ... suffered a sustained period of deep organisational trauma ... Financial pressures and cuts drove a cascade of multifarious organisational changes, which led to a dilution of the airworthiness regime and culture within the MoD, and distraction from safety

> ... There was a shift in culture and priorities in the MoD towards "business" and financial targets, at the expense of functional (military) values such as safety and airworthiness.[16]

Traditional military considerations associated with as airworthiness and equipment safety, in short, were the victims of the managerialist reform agenda sponsored by the government and promoted by the consultant. The report's author, Charles Haddon-Cave, also made comment of a culture of selfishness, reward and self-referenced promotion for change:

> Officers who effect "change" are more likely to be noticed and promoted ... There was a realisation by ambitious officers that being seen to initiate and effect "change" in post was good, or at least good for them. They would be perceived as "positive," "energetic," a "moderniser," a "person with good ideas," and "willing to try new things." The agents and apparatchiks of change gained quicker promotion.[17]

It seems that, as well as the government, the officers of the Royal Air Force in the UK had embraced the consultant's modernising agenda, aligning themselves to its ambition and intent, pursuing managerialist, homogenised change with the burning zeal of the recently converted. The management consulting profession, on the face of it, appears implicated in the consequences of this change.

The global practice of McKinsey & Co. has thrived since it was formed in 1923. Today, the company has an unrivalled reputation for excellence and expertise, employing over four thousand people globally, embracing pretty much every business sector. It is an extremely successful and well-respected consulting business. But the second point to note from Rasiel's book is just how repetitive and relatively uncreative the work was within the organisation. He discusses the daily grind of data sifting and interviews to populate pre-conceived management and operating models intended to diagnose and explain organisational problems. The models, not surprisingly, were portable from one organisation and sector to another. In fact this very portability was touted as proof of their worth and infallibility. This work was labour intensive, all-consuming and involved being away from home for much of the time and relied heavily on developing expertise through data-mining, information gathering and analysis, the very skills prized at the base of the management consulting profession. There was also significant competition between individual consultants and across consulting teams that hints at a practice riddled with rivalries rather than the collegiate workplace articulated by the consultancies themselves.

Perhaps not surprisingly, working conditions for consultants can be gruelling. On top of long hours in the office and at client sites, McKinsey consultants, as examples of the profession, would inevitably spend a large proportion of their time undertaking business travel, away from home, family and friends. I can testify that constant travelling for commercial reasons is far from fun, and commuting to work by aircraft may seem glamorous but can certainly take a heavy toll, not just on relationships, but on the very health of the consultant.

Survival or "sanity" techniques are, therefore, critical to enable a consultant to function appropriately and survive the profession as a reasonably healthy, decent human being, still cherished by her or his partner. Some consultants use their time stuck in a hotel room in a strange, distant city from home to learn a new language or other skill. Some become dedicated tourists visiting and viewing the sites of every city, town or business park they happen to be in. Whilst these activities may vary, consultants seem unified in the approach they take to working on the road. The first rule is to pack light in a small, portable suitcase that can be wheeled as "carry-on" luggage into an aircraft. Very few consultants have time or the patience to wait for a piece of luggage to be dragged from the bowels of an aeroplane to a luggage carousel. Flying with hand luggage only is a consummate skill: three shirts and underwear only packed, business suit worn, one document pack carried along with a laptop—that's it. For myself, I could work thousands of miles from home for months at a time, in the Middle East for instance, based on this simple guidance.

The practice of management consultancy attracts individuals who, typically, have a good university or business school education, are ambitious, inquisitive, paradoxically seem to like both chaos and structure, and are hugely competitive. Those who survive and thrive are smart, striving and lucky. Talking to younger consultants it is striking just how few recognised the hierarchical nature of their careers before making the fateful choice to become a consultant.[18] Such a consideration seems to have taken a number by surprise and is a driver for some to leave the profession early into their careers. This, in turn perhaps, prompts the thought that maybe management consultancy also attracts smart loners, men and women who like to unlock a set of problems through their own intellectual efforts but reject notions of corporate competitiveness. I recognise this trait in myself, an outsider, never destined to sit comfortably in any organisation mid to long-term.

Given this sense of consultancy as a blend of practices, activities, beliefs and explanations, I turn in Section Two to my own role as one of these consulting "experts" as a reflective and self-critical review of the significance of management consultancy.

Before exploring my own memories I quickly consider, in the next chapter, the notions of complexity and geopolitical uncertainty, and wonder how consultancy can possibly have the answers to management questions posed in a contingent, volatile and fast-shifting world.

Notes

1. I write about this difficulty of definition in my earlier work. See, for example, John Louth, *A Low Dishonest Decade: Smart Acquisition and Defence Procurement into the New Millennium* (Cardiff: UWIC, 2010).
2. See S. Child, *British Management Thought* (London: Allen & Unwin, 1964).
3. See Peter Drucker, *People and Performance* (London: Heinemann, 1977).
4. See F. Taylor, *The Principles of Scientific Management* (New York: Harper, 1911).
5. See Henry Fayol, *General and Industrial Management* (London: Pitman, 1949).
6. See H. Simon, *Administrative Behaviour* (London: Macmillan, 1960).
7. See Henry Mintzberg, "Strategy Making in Three Modes," *California Management Review* 16.2 pp. 44-53 and his myriad books on management and strategy.
8. See John Kotter, *Organisations and Leadership* (London: Collins, 1996).
9. See R. Stewart, *Choices for the Manager* (New Jersey: Prentice Hall, 1982).
10. See Sugata Biswas and Daryl Twitchell, *Management Consulting: A Complete Guide to the Industry* (New York: John Wiley & Sons, 2002).
11. Data sourced from the International Institute for Strategic Studies, *The Military Balance 2011, The Annual Assessment of Global Military Capabilities and Defence Economics* (London: Routledge, 2011).
12. See the Kennedy Information Research Group, *The Global Management Consulting Marketplace: Key Data, Forecasts and Trends, 2001* (New York: KIRG, 2001).
13. Biswas and Twitchell, op. cit., p. 21.
14. I conducted a number of semi-structured interviews with consulting practitioners during 2012 and 2013 which assisted with this analysis.
15. See Ethan M. Rasiel, *The McKinsey Way* (New York: McGraw-Hill, 1998).
16. Charles Haddon-Cave, *The Nimrod Review. An Independent Review into the broader issues surrounding the loss of RAF Nimrod MR2 XV230 in Afghanistan in 2006* (London: The Stationery Office, 2009) p. 12.
17. Ibid., p. 561.
18. Once more, semi-structured interviews and conversations with management consultants and their clients helped to develop this argument.

2. Global Complexity and Uncertainty—"No One Can Understand This!"

Complications

Whilst operating for much of my recent professional life in a consulting business that dealt in certainties and a causal relation between "problem" and "solution," I have always considered the world to be a complicated and often unyielding place; in fact, much more complicated and nuanced than the typical management consulting engagement would admit. As the writer Charles Handy[1] argues, we live in a challenging epoch where this sense of uncertainty is constant and endemic. Yet our intellectual and emotional responses often deter robust debate around exploring and understanding both an international scene and often a singular business of such puzzling complexity. Society's discourses and explanations lurch from one fashionable theory to another, encased within a myopic view of social structures, relationships and business conventions. These fashions, in turn, are embraced and promoted by the management consulting profession that imbue them with the tart flavours of "absolute diagnostic certainty" and "no alternative explanation." This results in intelligent and well-meaning people talking uncritically and with conviction and assurance of things such as "management," "markets," "strategy" and "governance" and applying such "thinking" to the business or reform of a project, a corporation or even an entire national function such as defence procurement.

Rather, it has always seemed to me, that both society and the individual are shaped by many different experiences, beliefs, values and ambitions making it difficult to promote trite explanations or simple models of explanation. Instead, as citizens and members of complex organisations, we all interact through a dynamic mix of strategies, policies, transactional processes, relationships and narratives to form and shape a highly fluid and contingent, multidimensional environment that often defies definition. For the policymaker, industrialist and corporate citizen alike, understanding that the topography and tides of this environment may be beyond reach is critical to our sense of well-being, especially in a time of budgetary constraint, macroeconomic retrenchment[2] and hoped for renewal. Such recognition, of course, does not help the management consultant develop his or her business. For them, all business or government factors must be knowable, explained or, at least, explainable.

Spaces

In contrast, I believe that there are a number of distinct geographical or "spatial" levels through which this modern environment may be glimpsed and conceptualised that seems beyond the current consulting toolbox: what I describe as the global, the regional, the "national" and the local. By this I mean the predisposition to see commercial and governmental activities, especially the transformation market favoured by consultants, as a global phenomenon, a regional endeavour, the preserve of a particular state, or a set of occurrences at a local level within a specific country.[3] There is a tension, however, in generating a clear understanding of the relationships between these four paradigms due, in no small part, to differences in scale, systemic complexity and a lack of comparative data. Moreover, the insights or lessons superficially gleaned from one level tend to contradict those from another, as this interaction does not lend itself to simple analysis. What does this mean for national and corporate leadership's capacity for decision-making and, correspondingly, for an organisation's ability to generate and sustain effective functional transformation or market traction? Without this more nuanced, elegant and contingent understanding, is there even a sensible management consulting value proposition?

This is not just abstract theorising. Taking the example of the United Kingdom, a place where I do much of my work, the significance of this sense of complexity starts to resonate. First, the United Kingdom is at a pivotal, strategic moment, the like of which it has not witnessed for perhaps generations.[4] The policy choices the government takes in response could well define the country's place in the world for the rest of the century and even shape and refine notions of statehood, citizenship and economic prosperity. Second, the commercial strategies of many corporate entities within the nation's industrial and commercial base are already being shaped in response to declining national revenues and budgets, reducing commitments and short-term state decision-making. Understanding the limits to our grasp on the tensions between a global perspective, regional ambitions, a set of state responsibilities and local economic and social impacts and interests, can help frame and illuminate these choices and the inevitable trade-offs and consequences they comprise. But the advisory profession, at least in my experiences, deals in certainty and not subtlety or nuance: the message that there are limits to our understanding and influence is less compelling than the promises of the absolute delivery of outcomes offered by the consultant.

Let me explore this further by offering one or two definitions. For "global" I am, of course, referring to the worldwide forces, factors, features and relationships—both formal and informal—that constitute the international geopolitical and interdependent economic system. It embraces state actors, state-sponsored international organisations, multinational corporations and their (often local) supply chains, other non-state actors and influencers, consumers, commentators and all other labels that can be applied to humankind. It is, by its very definition, a concept that is broad, inclusive and embracing of the whole world—though, in recent times (up to now at least) homed in the policy preferences and discourses of one nation-state—the United States—that enjoys hegemony over it.

I use "regional" as a term to indicate a group of states bound together through geography, international law, treaties, formal and informal alliances, and collective behaviours so that they can be conceptualised as a single (though, perhaps, multi-voiced) entity or market. This leads to a definition of the term "national" or, more properly, state. By "state" I mean a recognised community of people of mainly common descent, language and history, formed within a bounded area of governance with clear, though permeable, territorial borders. This level embraces anything that is peculiar to or characteristic of a particular state or country.

"Local," therefore, is concerned with a distinct and particular place, or places, for example within the UK state or the Indian nation. The sense of "local" is one bounded by geographical features, socio-economic factors, notions of identity (or multiple identities) and even local history. These four spatial areas collude to make the world subject to multiple narratives, explanations and meanings, offering a complex operating environment that is all but impenetrable. Overlaying these factors is, of course, the modern phenomenon of globalisation.

A Word on Globalisation

Globalisation is a contested term, used frequently, though often lazily, by political actors, industrialists and commentators alike. As management consultancy is perceived rightly as a global phenomenon, it seems sensible to grapple with a coherent definition, especially as:

> Since its earliest appearance in the 1960s, the term "globalisation" has been used in both popular and academic literature to describe a process, a condition, a system, a force and an age. Given that these competing labels have very different meanings, their indiscriminate usage is often obscure and invites confusion.[5]

Consequently, globalisation as a term can prove tricky to conceptualise as a conflation of process and condition serves only to offer circular definitions devoid of real explanatory force. Rather, we could use the term "globality" to signify a social *condition* dominated by the economic, political, environmental and cultural interdependencies and transactions that make irrelevant real and virtual borders and barriers. "Globalisation," therefore, can be defined as the set of social, economic, political and cultural *processes* that, combined, are transforming, and set to further transform, our present social and economic condition into one of globality.[6]

It is helpful as a consequence to think of globalisation as four interdependent and overlapping procedural entities. First, there is the creation of new, and multiplication of existing, social networks and occurrences that override traditional political, economic, geographical and cultural boundaries. Second, we could focus on the expansion and elasticity of social relations and interdependencies from the local to the international. Third, globalisation is characterised by the intensification and acceleration of social and economic exchanges and, fourth, there is the sense of a multiplication and intensification of subconscious socio-psychological interconnections and interdependencies between people and groups that were, somehow, previously disconnected.[7]

Today, the financial markets stretch around the planet and electronic trading and transfers of global capital never cease. Gigantic western-style shopping centres have developed on all continents offering consumers commodities from all corners of the world. Brands are recognised in outlets thousands of miles apart and new technologies and economic deregulation have shrunk the world so that what was once global has now become local. Moreover, the internet relays distant and sometimes complex information and imagery in seconds with real-time pictures of once far-off events. Local occurrences and values are shaped by events happening many miles away and vice versa, meaning that the seemingly opposing forces of globalisation and localisation actual self-implicate and reaffirm their importance to each other. So that, for me, the "global" and the "local" are mere endpoints of a spectrum that has the "regional" and the "national" as midpoints.[8] I would gently suggest that there are few working consultants today who even think about the world in this way.

Indeed, our planet can be said to have been compressed physically by globalisation through things such as technological advances and transport links. But it is also shrunk subconsciously and internally within the realm of the individual as forces of globalisation invade and reform the subjective sphere of human consciousness.[9] People at once remote from each other are increasingly aware of social and economic interdependencies and interactions so that the far away becomes near, personal and relevant. This sense of the receding importance of geography and distances engenders a keen conception of becoming part of a global, interdependent whole. And through constant, overt and subliminal reinforcement these persistent experiences and messages of global coherence and interconnectivity gradually invade and shape individual and collective identities. As such, globalisation becomes a multidimensional set of social, economic and psychological forces that create, multiply, stretch and intensify global interdependencies and exchanges enabling deeper connections between the local and the distant. Consequently, the impact of the process of globalisation and the formation of one "globality" is profoundly significant to the international system, between the macro and micro points across our spatial levels, but also to the individual actors that form it, such as the industrialist, worker, consumer and regulator. It does not lend itself to glib, simplistic analyses or "one-size-fits-all" consulting interventions as it defies simple explanation. Moreover, what I describe as the geopolitical, economic and social trends beyond 2020 only add to this sense of complexity and uncertainty.

International Trends—2020 and Beyond

Taking as our premise the sense that the "global" and "local" are endpoints of a continuum that has "regional" and "state" as distinct and separate levels in the middle of the spectrum, there are a number of significant trends and issues that feature commonly across all four levels, although their impacts, especially on the industrial and political decision-maker, vary depending upon the perspective and transaction being considered. These trends, in turn, form the backdrop to the operating environment faced by management consultants the world over. The five—what I would describe as "strategic"—trends that I wish to focus on are characterised under the headings of scale, the digital revolution, population and economic shifts, identity politics and climate change.

First, by scale I am simply referring to the sense drawn from the notion of globalisation that the world seems perceptively smaller in the modern epoch than in preceding eras. The effects of distance have shrunk significantly due to high-speed, affordable travel and communications. My virtual neighbour may live thousands of miles from my home, but I can engage with him or her instantly through social media and digital innovations. This increasingly undermines the autonomy of states and corporations as the effects of national and corporate policies diminish whilst events in the international arena often have great consequences for social and economic cohesion within the state. The strain, therefore, between international interdependence, at almost every level of human interaction and discourse, and state, national or corporate decision-making autonomy is an evolving strategic trend. Given this, consultants cannot be sure that the transformational processes that may be diagnosed for an organisation can possibly deliver the outputs of outcomes sought. The causal change models of the management consultant are increasingly redundant.

Second, and intrinsically implicated in the first, greatly improved technological capabilities for processing, carrying, transferring, storing and communicating information and data represent a truly transformative course of events. In the digital age we all dwell in a single cyber city where real-time information is both available to all and can be created by all, shaping responses to events and threats but also leading to significant structural and digital vulnerabilities for both businesses and countries alike. There is even the potential for new frontlines and conflicts associated with occurrences such as cyber attacks.

Third, populations in some parts of the world are increasing whilst others are stabilising and some shrinking, leading to tensions around the generation and use of human resources as both consumer and producer. Transnational migration seems a constant feature, and increasing and changing demands for raw materials, energy, foodstuffs and water represent a significant challenge to world order in the twenty-first century. Indeed, Chris Huhne, a previous Secretary of State for Energy and Climate Change in the United Kingdom, argued that food demand will grow globally by 20 per cent by 2050, itself a major trend for driving future conflicts.[10]

The fourth strategic trend is identity politics whereby, paradoxically, the trends of globalisation and communication reformation are accompanied by a desire to accentuate local identity (perhaps, even multiple local identities), or identity of place of origin. Within states, the stressing of identity or belonging can take the form of political "ethnicisation" that can threaten the fabric of the host society, as well as the projection of identity politics through religious affiliation. This is significant strategically for, "in the extreme, identity politics can form a breeding ground for radicalisation and ... terrorism."[11]

Lastly, global climate change is, potentially, a major strategic trend within the modern, globalised, industrialised and developing world. Whilst there are diverging views on the causes of climate change and the consequences of implementing mitigating strategies and plans, there is some agreement that average global temperatures are increasing.[12] The impacts of this continuing trend could range from food shortages, floods and droughts leading to mass streams of refugees and resource conflicts, through to a permanent shortage of materials essential to modern and developing economies.

The hazards or risks that these strategic trends give rise to can be classified schematically under headings of interstate conflicts;

materials and energy shortages; weapons of mass destruction; digital vulnerabilities; irregular conflict and terrorism; fragile states; cross-border crime and, finally, shocks associated with natural disasters.[13] I shall, shortly, come on to deal with each of these in turn.

By way of contrast, for the UK, the National Security Strategy (NSS)[14] of 2010 produced a list of self-styled threats to the country. The four most serious were assessed as international terrorism; cyber attacks; international military crises; and major accidents or natural occurrences. At the bottom of the list of threats were conventional military attacks on the UK or its dependencies, disruptions to oil and gas supplies as a result of conflict, and major political upheavals. These supposedly lesser threats, with lower probability and/or impact assessments, are precisely the issues being faced by the UK in this decade as evidenced by the country's involvement in the conflict in Libya and national and international responses to the phenomenon of the "Arab Spring." Consequently, some politicians and commentators are questioning whether the UK's NSS is sufficiently sophisticated and insightful to address the levels of complexity and uncertainty within the international system.

As presently conceived, the NSS fails to appreciate the complexity and unpredictability of modern threats. The networked world in which we now live affords the UK particular advantages, but also amplifies risks and vulnerabilities.[15]

Therefore, within this example, the UK sense of strategy may be challenged as to whether it has recognised the importance of preparing not just for what can be anticipated through the lens of risk management within the NSS but, much more significantly, for those strategic risks and shocks that cannot. Needless to say, the policy responses of politicians in the United Kingdom have been informed and flavoured by a number of the international management consulting businesses operating in London.

Hazards, Risks and Shocks

For now, let us consider the hazards, risks and even the potential shocks that predominate. Whilst global conflict and total war between states appear receding phenomena, there remain dormant territorial conflicts, such as Kashmir, that could escalate into open conflict. Moreover, shifts in the power relationship between major states—the emergence of China relative to the US, for example—could be a cause of future conflicts. Of course, rival states do not have to limit themselves to the classic instruments of war but may pose irregular threats and sponsor cyber attacks.

Shortages of raw materials and energy sources also pose a considerable hazard. The economic development of Asia, the wider Pacific region, South America and the states of the Indian Ocean, all collide and collude in the contestation of scarce and finite materials. There are rival claims for energy stocks and means of transport, and transport routes themselves are increasingly constrained. A strategic shock associated with, perhaps, a blockade through the Strait of Hormuz is far from inconceivable.

Issues around weapons of mass destruction—nuclear, biological, chemical or radiological—pose a distinct and terrifying set of hazards. These can derive from the proliferation of formal, state-sponsored programmes through to the manufacture of ad hoc "dirty bombs," but the outcome of such an attack could be a significant strategic shock. So would the realisation of threats associated with the vulnerability of communication and information networks and the hazards of digital paralysis, along with the standing threats of irregular combat methods and terrorism. Coupled with the perils posed by fragile and failing states, organised cross-border crime and the ever-present capacity for shocks caused by natural disasters and environmental events, all of these hazards contextualise and populate a challenging operational environment in which to make sense of the world. We can only properly understand and discuss our place in the world today—whether at a global level, through a regional perspective, within the state or locally—through the lens of these, and other, hazards and shocks. For the certainties of yesterday:

> ... have given way to a new kind of geopolitical environment where there are fewer threats ... but many more risks. These are in many ways more numerous, more diverse, less easily identifiable and, as a consequence, less easily countered.[16]

A response to this level of complexity calls for humility and contingency at the expense of absolute certainty. This is profoundly challenging to the management consulting profession.[17]

A Global Perspective

From the Reformation to the second part of the twentieth century, Europe was at the centre of the international system, its empires generating a single "global" domain possibly for the first time in history. The principal trade route, and bridge from Europe to the wider world, was naturally the North Atlantic. Through these waters the basic topography of global politics was formed and fused into place. However, from 1945 onwards that global international system has been subtly transforming. For the first time in the modern epoch transatlantic trade has been equalled, and then eclipsed, by transpacific trade, so that:

> With Europe reduced to a collection of secondary powers after World War II, and the shift in trade patterns, the North Atlantic was no longer the single key to anything. Now whatever country controlled both the North Atlantic and the Pacific could control ... the world's trading system, and therefore the global economy. In the twenty-first century, any nation located on both oceans has a tremendous advantage.[18]

North America, consequently, has replaced Europe at the epicentre of the international political and economic system. Whoever dominates North America is virtually assured of being the primary global power of the early years of the twenty-first century. The global level, therefore, is characterised by US hegemony, with US ambitions and fears its dominant attributes. This is not to say that the US is not challenged by traditional competitors and emerging powers, it is, and will undoubtedly be tested by rival states in the years to come. Yet for now there is but one global, though fading, superpower, the US, and it dominates the international economic and political system.[19] A system, of course, that is grappling with the forces of globalisation and possessed of significant hazards and threats, but one in which the notion of globality is explicitly American flavoured. But for now only: China, a resurgent Russia, the economic powerhouse that is India and the potential of Brazil will challenge this American hegemony throughout this century and continually shrink and reshape it.[20]

By way of a day job I write and speak about defence and security. I want now to divert into a brief discussion of the defence industrial base and US policy imperative as a way of exploring this international complexity and notion of uncertainty. As a way of addressing these risks and vulnerabilities that exist globally, a capable and secure defence industrial sector is perceived in the US as a strategic national asset contributing significantly to the slippery concepts of US political power, military might and the continuance of global hegemony.[21] As Ashton B. Carter, the erstwhile US Under-Secretary of Defence for Acquisition, Technology and Logistics has stated:

> A strong, technologically vibrant and financially successful defence industry is ... in the national interest. In this respect the warfighter's and taxpayer's interest are fundamentally aligned with ... industry.[22]

Driven in part by this policy insight, as well as in response to a growing US fiscal deficit, Carter and fellow US senior leaders have increasingly championed the promotion of a new American defence industrial strategy which, of course, has significant global implications.[23] This response, nuanced and contingent on world events and perceived global trends, as far as I can tell, was developed without the overt use of management consultants.

The emerging US strategy recognises that both government and wider society have an enduring interest in the maintenance and promotion of the US defence industrial base as critical national capability to promote and enable global stability. This seems to be yielding a growing national consensus on developing policies and processes that will secure long-term innovation and productivity, offering solutions that are both profitable for the industrialist and economically efficient for the taxpayer.

Let us follow this example for a moment. At the heart of this refreshed defence industrial strategy in America, US leaders wish to rely on the utility of classic market forces to initiate enduring structural adjustments to the defence industrial base. The confluence of global capital markets, technological innovations, intellectual creativity and government consumer confidence will deliver a sustainable and globally dominant defence industrial base, or so the policymakers believe. Moreover, as competition is thought to be the principal enabler of economic prosperity, US policy does not extend to the further consolidation or rationalisation of principal weapons systems prime contractors or other dominant industrial actors.

Significantly, US defence industrial policy is also focused on the economic layer below the prime contractors, as US policymakers believe that smaller firms and new entrants are liable to generate new solutions and refreshed technologies, so offering battlefield advantages and commercial efficiencies. This is especially important for service sector companies as about half of all defence contracts by value in the US go to service providers rather than the more traditional defence equipment manufacturers. This focus on service companies as incubators of innovation is at the centre of the US commitment to review and revamp its industrial base through each defence capability area, from aircraft manufacturing to small arms and ammunition. When each capability area and sector is "right-sized" and "right-shaped" the US government is committed to developing policies, processes and commercial incentives to secure, sustain and protect it.[24]

As the dominant global actor, the US commitment to its defence industrial base, whether truly indigenous or adopted and absorbed, will ensure that the US remains vigilant and potentially ready to address unidentified and unknown strategic shocks, and prepared for the unprecedented pressures that such shocks place on policymakers and wider society. The world has predicted few, if any, of the military conflicts it has witnessed since the end of the Second World War[25] and it seems that, in part, the US has drawn an uncomplicated insight from this: a full spectrum of forces backed by a robust industrial base and appropriate national investment is strategically critical as the world navigates through the choppy waters of the era of uncertainty.

The policy initiative in the US on the durability, size, shape and purpose of the defence industrial base to support this full spectrum of military responses has now begun, with industry and commerce seen as critical national resources and sources of power. This offers opportunities to non-US corporations as the Obama Administration seems committed to reducing barriers to market entry and, where appropriate, embracing new entrants, both to the US and operating from the US. The question is whether non-US corporate leaders are open to these opportunities, understand how to shape them, and how attuned they were in the first place to these shifting global sands. This last question implicates the many consulting advisers working with these organisations.

This is a complicated discussion. The point to be made to conclude this section is that management consultancy in its modern iteration is predicated on the predictable, linear diagnosis which yields common responses and tick-box interventions. It trades in certainty. The world, as I describe it above, is contingent, complex, uncertain and constantly changing. Within management consultancy today we may be witnessing the promotion of an analogue solution packaged for a post-digital world. The dangers of this we can only guess as we come on to explore in the next section common themes of consultancy, the products, if you like, of the profession, and the core idea of expertise that can be packaged, marketed and sold.

Notes

1. Charles Handy, *The Hungry Spirit* (London: Arrow, 1998).
2. Malcolm Chalmers, "The Lean Years: Defence Consequences of the Fiscal Crisis," in Michael Codner and Michael Clarke (eds.), *A Question of Security:*

The British Defence Review in an Age of Austerity (London: I.B. Tauris, 2011), pp. 33-75.

3. Henrik Heidenkamp, John Louth and Trevor Taylor, *The Defence Industrial Ecosystem: Delivering Security in an Uncertain World* (London: Stephen Austin and Sons, 2011). ISSN 1750-9432, p 13
4. Michael Clarke, "The United Kingdom's Strategic Moment," in Michael Codner and Michael Clarke (eds.), *A Question of Security: The British Defence Review in an Age of Austerity* (London: I.B. Tauris, 2011), pp. 7-19.
5. See Manfred Steger, *Globalisation* (Oxford: OUP, 2003) p. 7.
6. See Anthony Giddens, *Runaway World* (Cambridge: Polity Press, 2000).
7. For a useful summary of these issues see Roland Robertson, *Globalisation* (Oxford: OUP, 1992).
8. Manfred Steger, op. cit., p. 11.
9. Michel Foucault, *Discipline and Punish* (London: Allen Lane, 1963).
10. Speaking at the Royal United Services Institute for Defence and Security Studies' (RUSI) Annual Maritime Conference, July 7, 2011.
11. Netherlands Ministry of Defence, *Strategic Knowledge Agenda* (The Hague: MoD, 2009) p. 15.
12. John Houghton, *Global Warming—The Complete Briefing* (New York, NY: Cambridge University Press, 2009).
13. Netherlands Ministry of Defence, *Strategic Knowledge Agenda* (The Hague: MoD, 2009) pp. 8-11.
14. National Security Strategy, 2010.
15. Bernard Jenkin MP and George Grant, *The Tipping Point: British National Strategy and the UK's Future World Role* (London: The Henry Jackson Society, 2011) p. 23.
16. Ibid., p. 14.
17. Throughout 2012 and 2013 I interviewed a number of partners and directors of management consulting businesses. The overriding impression was that the profession struggles with complexity.
18. George Friedman, *The Next 100 Years* (London: Allison and Busby Ltd., 2010) p. 20.
19. Lisa Aronsson, "Strategic Considerations for the Anglo-American Alliance," in Michael Codner and Michael Clarke (eds.), *A Question of Security: The British Defence Review in an Age of Austerity* (London: I. B. Tauris, 2011), pp. 79-90.
20. See, for example, Eric J. Weiner, *The Shadow Market: How Sovereign Wealth Funds Secretly Dominate the Global Economy* (Oxford: Oneworld Publication, 2011).
21. Heidenkamp et al., op. cit., p. 10.
22. Ashton B. Carter (Undersecretary of Defence for Acquisition, Technology and Logistics), speaking at the Cowen Investment Conference, New York, NY, February 9, 2011.
23. US Department of Defence, *Better Buying Power: Guidance for Obtaining Greater Efficiency and Productivity in Defence Spending*, memorandum for acquisition professionals, September 2010.

24. Robert Gates (US Secretary for Defence), speech to NATO Strategic Concepts Seminar, National Defence University, Washington, DC, February 23, 2010.
25. Bernard Jenkin and George Grant, op. cit., p. 23.

SECTION TWO

3. My Role as "An Expert"

All Is Not as It Seems

As we have seen from the preceding section, there are (at the very least) two interesting phenomena occurring in relation to management consultancy and the interdependent global economic and geopolitical systems. First, we have dominating features of immense global complexity, uncertainty and even disorder. Second, we have an international management consulting market that is thriving on the promotion of diagnostic certainty despite this complicated modern state. This is fascinating, and whilst on first sight many people might consider that these two conditions are mutually exclusive, in my view management consultancy makes a virtue of this tension. For example, my own consulting career was undertaken contextually to offer management coherence in response to complexity, so that my promotion of the managerially certain and obvious was viewed as a way of taming and controlling the wild and uncertain. This took the form of me being sold-out to clients as an "expert" in transformation and change management, risk and opportunity management, programme management and recovery and corporate strategy, to name but a few activities I undertook. The following chapters address each of these four areas in some detail using an appropriate example or multiple examples from my professional life; but before this I wish to dwell on this concept of expertise as it goes right to the heart of the management consulting idea and business value proposition.

The Expert and Management Consultancy

Each consultancy organisation sells their staff to their clients as subject-matter experts. It could hardly be otherwise, as I have never heard, as yet, of an organisation buying the time of a consultant on the basis that he or she had merely a rough idea of what they were doing and were partially qualified. So, at the very heart of the consulting concept is the transfer of expertise from the consultant to the client via the selling of the expert's time. From what I have seen to date, there are indeed a number of very well qualified and experienced consultants who excel at making the sale and perhaps even supervise the consulting engagement. I would even concede that such individuals are excellent at managing the relationship with their client through a mixture of charm, personality, past credibility and the strength of the consulting brand they represent. But much of the actual work within the engagement—the diagnosis and analysis to use Rasiel's terms, the development of options to generate the client's required outcomes, and even the making of recommendations—is left to more junior staff.

For example, during my time in the Middle East, working in partnership with one of the largest global consulting brands, the managing partner from this business directed the relationship with the client but left all of the detailed work to a junior analyst. It was clear that this analyst was a good and conscientious young professional, but he had neither the past customer experiences nor the skills to develop an emerging solution to meet the demands of a nervous client. Consequently we ended up with a stew of past financial models and organisational analyses cut and pasted from previous engagements, being hastily put together at the last minute by the team and applied to the current client's circumstances. This was shamelessly offered by the consulting partner under the badges of "learning from experience" and "best practice" which, at the very least, seems disingenuous.

That the advisory business in question could get away with this has something to do with the notion and place of "expertise" in the mindset of the client and the brand strength of the consulting practice. But, in truth, the expertise demonstrated was a trite and shallow expertise associated with relationship management, strong presentation skills and the ability to manage client meetings rather than subject-matter excellence.

Interestingly, each of us involved with that engagement was highly credentialised by our qualifications. I am an accountant and hold a number of different degrees and professional qualifications. We had lawyers and bankers with appropriate certificates also involved and this mix of professional credibility and hard-won qualifications offered much comfort to the client, even as the consulting partner briefed from rehashed presentations, drawing findings and conclusions from insights gleaned from previous engagements. The qualifications of the consulting team added to the allure of expertise but were not actually relevant to the core consulting practice of client management, as revealed through that engagement. What is truly fascinating, though, is that the client was thrilled having so many "experts" presenting to him, glorifying in the qualifications held, so was more than happy to pay for services received. The tale of yet another successful consulting engagement could, of course, be used by consultants to sell yet more services to this client and others whereby the roll-out of yet more expertise continues as almost an organic consequence of what has travelled before. After all, only a fool would argue with a record of expertise and success and no client or potential client wishes to be seen as a fool.

Making the Sale

The core skills of the seasoned and senior management consultant are business development and sales. All but the most junior consultants in practice have sales targets and a sure route to a reprimand or dismissal is failure to meet annual sales targets. Invariably this means that for a number of consultants securing the deal is the focus of their efforts rather than the detail of the client's perceived problem of their own skills and competencies in delivering an enduring solution. Unlike banking or financial services, misselling, as yet, is an alien concept to the management consulting profession. I believe that this will become a major industry theme during the next few years, especially as management consultancies grow into the service spaces traditionally provided by governments. Should this prediction prove correct, the governance of the consultancy profession, at national and international levels, will become a major societal issue. I return to this theme in latter chapters.

I make the case for the sales function being remarkably important to the consulting profession. This has been my experience in the market place both as practitioner and analyst. Yet many consultants will state forcefully and with passion that the firm they work for does not engage in sales.[1] Somehow, they might assert, selling their services seems to be below the dignity of a profession that has its roots in accountancy and engineering professional services. But, it seems clear that securing a client pitch and making a sale is the lifeblood of the consulting firm. Partners and directors have their remuneration packages developed to reflect the amount of business that they can bring to a practice. How can we reconcile this apparent difference in emphasis when it comes to the subject of selling?

It seems to me that the more prosperous and enduring consulting firms do not "cold call" potential client as some besuited double glazing salesman of myth might, but rather they market brilliantly so that the same potential client automatically calls in the consultancy when a business problem is identified or the necessity for change perceived. As part of this marketing effort, consulting companies might generate a continual pipeline of papers, articles, speeches and even books so that the consultant's individual expertise within a particular domain or business area is constantly stated, reinforced and validated by the effort itself. Firms like McKinsey and PA Consulting, for example, may produce their own quarterly journals for the use of existing, and as yet unidentified, clients and the wider business community. Such a consulting company will engage proactively with journalists, analysts in think tanks, legislators, their specialist advisers and so on, so that senior consultants become imbued with the pixie-dust of expertise and credibility. This methodology is a form of advanced "selling for professionals"—a form of sales through reputational positioning, business development, networking and branding that is as subtle and effective as it is omnipotent. A client's confirmation of an order is the inevitable, perhaps even unstoppable, consequence of these endeavours, signposting, in a way, the triumph of the sales process over other practices at the heart of the management consulting proposition. Its power over the industry should not be underestimated.

With this in mind, I now turn my gaze onto a number of consulting activities which seem to dominate the market in the twenty-first century. The practice of change management seems the appropriate place to begin.

Notes

1. A number of private interviews and conversations between 2011 and 1013 contributed to this analysis.

4. Transformation and Change Management

All Change

Management consultancy in almost every way is fundamentally about change. This might be structural, organisational, cognitive, emotional, technological or even physical. If it can be conceptualised and articulated, then the client's problem or inherent nervousness can be turned into a change programme by the skilled consultant. As a consequence, words such as "change" and "transformation" are at the very centre of the lexicon of consultancy. It could hardly be otherwise.

Change, however, is a double-edged management and social scientific phenomenon. It can help align an organisation to its strategy though, quite often, only in a limited sense, or it can unleash a wave of unrest, dissatisfaction and ill-considered impacts across an environment. Such a perfect storm, on occasions, can generate a tempest from which the business entity in question cannot be recovered. The point about change management as a discipline is that managerial outcomes are seldom certain and consequences can extend beyond those intended. As we discussed in earlier chapters, the world is a complicated, non-linear place beyond the rules of causation.

For much of my professional life I have been involved in designing change engagements and, on one occasion, with the development of a business consultancy's entire change management practice. Despite this, I still struggle to properly identify the objectives, practices or effects of change management *as a discipline* and how, when combined, these factors can yield the business benefits so often claimed.

One consultancy that I worked for was considering developing an overt change management methodology and toolset to enable the company to compete for, and win, high-value change management engagements. This was perceived to be a lucrative and sensible strategic choice for the company to make. In fact, more properly, if the company was not successful in acquiring a part of the booming change management market, senior consultants like me and my fellows would have failed to develop the business to its full potential. The task of aligning the business's competencies to its ambition to be a player in the transformation advisory business was given to me.

The Change Management Proposition

My first objective was to identify just what we meant by "change management" or "transformation." This was a relatively straightforward task. A quick reading of the business press and one or two management books quickly told me that, within business schools, change management as a concept is usually accessed and understood through three distinct areas of explanation and definition:

- The task of managing organisational and team change;
- An area of professional practice;
- An emerging intellectual body of knowledge.

The first and perhaps most obvious definition is that the term refers to the task of managing a specific, identified change. The obvious, however, is not necessarily unambiguous, as the management of change in this context has at least two meanings. The first is the introduction of changes to an organisation in a planned, managed and systematised manner within the control of an organisation. The second is the ad hoc response to changes generated from within the operating environment over which the organisation has little or no control. In part, driven by this tension, researchers, typically distinguish between a reactive change management response and an anticipative, planned initiative. The distinction is said to be important if the correct strategy is to be crafted by an organisation seeking to change.

In contrast, the area of professional practice associated with transformation and change management stretches from multinational partnerships operating at a global level through to niche, sole traders. Some claim to manage the consequences of inevitable changes, others to make desirable changes to operating procedures and bottom-line results. However, it is the claimed expertise in the task of managing the *process* of change that is the unique proposition in change management as a professional practice across consultancy. Understanding the process is the key to fully grasping the practice.

Third, there are the models, methods and techniques through which practitioners engage the marketplace that occupies the body of knowledge associated with change management. These, in turn, have been supplemented by, and interchanged with, the models and methods to be found in the business schools and other areas of academia, especially within the West. The content or subject matter is drawn from psychology, business administration, economics, industrial engineering, systems engineering and the study of human and organisational behaviour. Within a globalised environment, these component bodies of knowledge are linked and integrated by a set of concepts and principles that comprise a general systems theory of change.

When I was initially charged with developing a management consulting proposal for the development of a change management practice, I was not clear at all whether this area of practice should be seen as an integrated and mature profession, a discipline, an art or a technology. For the purposes of my organisation it was sufficient to point out that there was a large, cohesive but eclectic body of knowledge underpinning the practice of change management that many practitioners would find common ground with, even if their application of the principles would demonstrate a high degree of variance masquerading as client choice within the market.

The Change Management Body of Knowledge

It was clear to me, though, that this self-styled body of knowledge of change management was homed in the universities' business schools and that this pedagogy gave it a legitimacy and acceptability within society. Consequently this knowledge could be sifted, coded and "commodified," allowing the consultants to make money from change management. And, of course, this legitimisation and academic credibility remains at the heart of the consulting profession today. The practice of change management is a vignette of the wider consulting profession.

When I looked at this subject with the view to developing a change management practice for my business it was obvious that there were a number of leading, and fashionable, schools of thought and academics important to the practice of change management. These included Peter Senge and his work on the "learning organisation"; Ruth Cohn and "theme centred interaction"; Virginia Satir and "systems thinking"; Harrison Owen, Marvin Weisbord and their methodology for "whole systems change"; the practice of human resource management and personnel development; total quality management and other manufacturing and whole-systems practices.[1] An awareness and familiarity with the work of these thinkers and disciplines, of course, enabled a framed and bounded debate on the nature of change management and what its adoptive practices could yield to the company for which I worked. However, I could not resist the thought that there may well have been a myriad of other approaches and tools from other disciplines that potentially could have become fashionable in the future. Change management may not have been the elixir that many in my consultancy thought.

Nonetheless, at a practitioner level, the theory of change management seems important in providing hints and insights into organisational problems, and consultants frequently articulate the need for a structured, programmatic approach to the subject. I partly still share this view and, when I practised as a consultant, for me a change management contract was about analysing a team, an organisation or a process to address a number of simple, discernible problems or unrealised opportunities.

Problem-Solving: Change Management Diagnosis and Implementation

For my business, we sold change management solutions based on a framework for thinking about the change process as problem solving. Managing change was a matter of moving from one state to another, specifically from a problem state to a solved one. Diagnosis or problem solving was, therefore, essential in that at the heart of any change initiative was an understanding and agreement as to what is the actual problem. This process itself involved significant client engagement and stakeholder management using sales skills, negotiation techniques and diagnostic tools that are familiar to any trader from the dawn of time, not alchemy set within the preserve of a few, somehow, gifted consultants.

Within the practice we frequently articulated a problem by seeing something as a "how problem," a "what problem," or a "why problem." If the problem is "how do we get the team to produce more?" then we may naturally assume that higher production will solve the problem. If the problem, however, is "why are our profits falling?" then higher productivity may just be but one strategy to be considered amongst a range of options. Thus, chains and networks of ends-means relationships need to be thoroughly worked out before a problem state can be accurately described, let alone a solution articulated. The key point is that change management engagements seek to, first, state and capture the problem. Second, the preferred or so-called "solution state" must be clear and unambiguous. Only then can a change process be designed and implemented. This is, of course, reasonable and good sense, yet most clients accepted this as proof of the consultants' greater diagnostic and reasoning abilities. At one level, therefore, for the practice of consultancy, change management is a diagnostic and creative process. We now need to consider what the change process itself comprises, both in design and practice.

There is a whole library of books to describe how effective change should be implemented. This bulk of work can be distilled into a number of guiding principles, which most competent consultants possess. First and foremost, it is pivotal within a change engagement to increase the urgency for action. Specifically the consultant and senior managers must inspire people within the organisation to move by overtly articulating the problem and corresponding opportunity. Part of this dynamic is to create the reality that staying the same equates to failure, either organisational or personal, with all the consequences that may evolve.

Secondly, it seems important for consultants to build the guiding team within an engagement. This means getting the leadership and transformation team right, with the right mix of energy, emotional commitment, creativity, credibility and ability to stick with the change. To do this the consultant needs to sell his or her vision to the senior management within an organisation and key influencers within its ranks. Once more, sales skills come to the fore.

As part of our change management methodology my company felt that it was important to get the vision right from the beginning. To do this we would get the team in question to create a clear, unambiguous and simple vision of where the organisation needed to get. Simple was the word that we emphasised. It was clear from experience that if this vision was complex, interpretive, full of caveats or in some way nuanced or subtle the change engagement would fail. Keeping it simple, or simplistic, was the key to success. However, as we have seen from earlier chapters the real world is complex, multifaceted and unyielding to simple models of trite analyses. The quest for simplicity of practice is not in step with the complications of commercial, social and political environments.

Next, within my consulting organisation we urged our teams to communicate endlessly; to de-clutter communications and force the senior team within the client business to spend more time talking and reinforcing simple change management messages. In part this allowed the client to empower action within his or her organisation; to remove obstacles and caveats and to reward and recognise progress and achievements. In many ways, from the outset of our practice, we designed the potential for short-term wins by setting aims that could be measured and delivered early in the programme. Thereafter we ensured that the client's top team celebrated their achievement thereby reinforcing the success and importance of the change programme. The client would be coached to keep going, to encourage determination and commitment to the programme's end-state. In this way we would make change the day job and ongoing reality for all employees. Lastly, we would encourage the ability to make the change stick by recruiting and promoting those who embraced the required end-state, whose values and ambition matched those of the "new" organisation.

For all consulting practices the change programme in design and execution must address the issues I have just highlighted. In implementation they are brought to life through stated changes to an organisation or team's strategy, culture, use of technology, internal processes and distribution/engagement with current and emerging markets. A change may be required in just one of these areas, but they intertwine, and all must be factored into the change engagement if it is to be successful. Consultants often believe that a good way of doing just that is to consider the human aspect of organisations and change management though competence frameworks and maturity models. For example, people are said to possess value competencies, behavioural competencies, functional competencies and organisational competencies. Changing competencies through training, realignment of organisational processes and team values will, potentially, impact on an entity's culture, the way work is conducted, its use of technology and the way a team presents and delivers its products and deals with customers and the wider world. The trick is to design this approach into the change solution and pursue it without distraction or the troubling recognition that the world is more complicated than our models and explanations will allow.

But for the active management consultant the change management process is about an almost linear intellectual occurrence:

- Firstly, use diagnostic tools to "problematise" the issue through "why" "what" "how" analyses.
- Secondly, overtly and simply state the required end-state in organisational, team and individual terms.
- Thirdly, design the change engagement to satisfy the delivery of the required state—it is a creative, subjective process. By definition it's right, if it is organisationally derived.
- Lastly, implement through project management, sales and stakeholder engagement techniques.

This fourth stage was where my company thought it could, potentially, add enormous value to clients and differentiate itself in the change marketplace. The company's core competency was the effective management of programmes and projects. Change management was such a programme and could be presented as a number of change activities with a budget, resource, start date and planned conclusion. Consequently, for my business, this activity could be conceptualised and managed using the full toolset of project control techniques that overtly aid measurement, progress and delivery. My organisation recognised that a pervading criticism of change management engagements was that they could often be characterised as "soft" and imponderable. Our commercial opportunity was to argue that the best programmes were neither of these. Consequently, our unique selling point was to be the management of change engagements through project control disciplines thus providing a rigour throughout the self-styled change journey. In this way we could blend creativity with management science making us, we thought, stand out in the marketplace.

The problem for us at the time was that it was very difficult to gauge the actual size of the change management market. Simply, within the public sector in the UK, governmental reforms, macroeconomic tensions and public policy were driving the need for public organisations to become more effective, efficient and to deliver products and services in ever new ways. The Society of Procurement Officers estimated that the public sector change management market was £40 billion per annum in 2005. A proportion of this represented a significant prize for my company if we could secure a part of this market. Moreover, within industry and commerce in the UK, the amount spent on change management engagements was estimated at £22 billion per annum. Given that there were a number of large international private companies that fell beyond this analysis, we concluded that this market was one for us. Consequently, our sales effort, business development initiatives and recruitment strategies were all aligned to the imperative to secure a foothold in the change management market.

The key point was that this activity would be sales led rather than competency derived. This meant that we were blind to the very real constraints framing change management engagements. One of these key concerns is profoundly significant, namely just how successful can change management interventions actually be? It has always seemed to me that companies and public sector activities that enjoy long-term, sustained success and growth have at their heart a core purpose and set of values. These are fixed and do not, and should not, change. Corporate strategies and practices of course can adapt and morph into sensible responses to changing markets and broader environments, but the very soul of the organisation remains constant—at least if those charged with its stewardship wish it to be successful. This insight seems the antithesis of the premise for change management.

What may be needed today, therefore, is not uncritical change management peddled by the consultant but a rare and nuanced ability to balance adaptive continuity and change. But this, though, probably offers less of a commercial opportunity to change management practitioners and their investors.

Moreover, as change management is now an omnipresent phenomenon, organisations are full of managers and workers who are, what could be described as, "change survivors." These are people who have learnt to live through myriad change programmes and transformation agendas without actually changing themselves, their values or the way in which they do business. The presence of these people can make the efforts of those consulting on change management seem a distraction or a noise to be tuned-out, rendering the transformation process a pointless, though expensive, practice.

Consultants themselves may claim that such organisational difficulties and uncertainties can be managed through other engagements such as an effective risk and opportunity management roll-out, another rich seam of profitable practice for the management consultant. It is to this that we turn our attention in the next chapter.

Is It Really a Time for Change?

Is it really a time for change? As a final word, it now seems that change for many commercial and governmental organisations is the only constant. The drive to order and manage this change is a natural business imperative for leadership teams. But consensual, common diagnoses and responses do not lead to organisational differentiation or business success within the marketplace. How can they? If we just do the same as our competitors and join the dance of endless change management, the market becomes homogenised, uncritical and the antithesis of reflective practice, the very conditions that, I contend, lead to long-term failures. No doubt, as I write, consultants and their sales teams are developing propositions to address this very point. If so, change management may be seen to become part of the problem rather than a bold, managerial intervention.

Notes

1. For an excellent overview of the so-called learning organisation through systems' thinking please see Peter Senge, *The Fifth Discipline* (London: Random House, 1990).

5. Risk Management

The Value Proposition

A key element of the management consultant's "value proposition," which is a sales and delivery term I encountered frequently throughout my dalliance with the consulting profession, is this sense of deliberately capturing and managing the risks to an organisation, or to a specific programme or project. As a consequence, Risk and Opportunity Management, as a practice, is a rich and fertile ground for management consultants to enjoy, and I undertook many consulting engagements to insert a risk management system into an entity as part of an organisational or project governance regime, or to independently undertake a risk, opportunity and uncertainty review. This is a phenomenon that needs a little investigation. Just what do we actually mean by risk management and how does a project team, for example, utilise the practices of risk and opportunity management to deliver stated goals, benefits and organisational objectives?

The Project Team

To dig into this question, kindly allow me to introduce you to the EPCOT project team.[1] This project team was a group of about 150 civil servants and military officers and managers, based predominantly at the United Kingdom's Defence Logistics Organisation's air headquarters near St. Ives in Cambridgeshire. Members of staff were also located throughout the industry base around the United Kingdom, Europe, and beyond, whilst the military belonging to the project team were often to be found on Royal Air Force operating bases, mostly in the south of the UK. The project team was led by a group captain and had a small management board of five directors, including the team leader, embracing primarily commercial, financial and engineering functions.

The EPCOT project team existed to "provide optimised logistic support to a safe and effective operational fleet." To do this it generated, through commercial relationships with industry, design, maintenance, repair and disposal services to four aircraft types flown by the Royal Air Force (RAF). The project team, following an earlier engagement with management consultants, freely used the word "customer" within its management documentation and narrative explanations when describing the Royal Air Force. The team, therefore, in its own language, provided serviceable aircraft to its front-line customer, the Royal Air Force, to undertake military missions as required by the government of the United Kingdom and its allies. It generated these aircraft by entering into detailed service contracts with public and private companies both within the United Kingdom and abroad, based upon commercial principles and processes, as available at that time. In doing this, the project team directed the spending of significant, multi-million dollar sums on industry maintenance contracts for the types of aircraft it supported.

I was contracted as a management consultant to assist this project team with the insertion of a risk management analysis and review structure, with associated managerial processes, across all of its fleets of aircraft. It involved working with both the project team and the commercial businesses holding its contracts. The casual observer within the UK, at this time in 2006, using her or his own common sense and intuition, would probably suggest that military technicians and engineers maintained and serviced

Royal Air Force aircraft. This imagined, a casual observer would point to documentaries and newsreel clips showing uniformed tradesmen working on fighter aircraft and bombers as part-evidence of this assertion. But that was not the case then and is most definitely not the case today.

Rather, the large maintenance and servicing programmes and schedules of work are provided by industry. In the case of the EPCOT project team, a publicly traded FTSE 100 company and a private business provided the maintenance, repair and overhaul contracts for the Royal Air Force fleets supported by the project team. So, in a glib manner, perhaps, but certainly pregnant with poignancy, symbolism and meaning, the military in the form of the project team wrote the cheques and wished to perform exercises in due diligence and risk management whilst industry maintained and delivered the military aircraft. The project team was the oversight entity specialising in the practices of management, such as the new requirement for risk oversight; industry, in contrast, was the service and engineering function to the front line.

The project team wanted to contribute to its decision-making through what it described as a risk and opportunity management *process*, extracted specifically from project management principles and methodologies. As Burke states[2]

> A key component of change is making decisions—ideally these decisions would be based on complete information with a high degree of certainty of the outcome. However, in the real world most decisions are based in incomplete information with an associated level of uncertainty about the outcome—it is this uncertainty that leads to risk. So risk has always been an intrinsic part of project management. It can be seen that risk, uncertainty and opportunity are closely related. When a risk occurs, with some

> entrepreneurial ingenuity, this may be turned around to become an opportunity, and conversely when pursuing an opportunity there will be associated risks.

Indeed, the EPCOT project team's head of department, Wing Commander de Coverley, explained to me during lengthy discussions that the successful management of the project team's risk and uncertainty was one of the primary project management principles that would determine the timely completion of programmes within clearly defined, understood and agreed timescales. He believed that what he described as "risk modelling" against an indicative "high-level" risk schedule would generate effective project delivery dates, cost profiles and schedule impacts, thereby ensuring a productive and useful air fleet.

De Coverley went on to explain that a common risk management framework had been adopted by the EPCOT project team, with project risk being defined as:

> ... an uncertain event or condition that, if it occurs, has a positive or negative effect on a programme objective.

Accordingly, practices of risk and opportunity management, the project team believed, maximises a project's chances of achieving its cost, schedule and performance objectives by identifying areas of uncertainty. The process proposes methods and activities whereby risks can be reduced, opportunities exploited, and, thereafter, a management team can implement and monitor derived risk and opportunity action plans. Once these risks have been identified against project objectives, they can be assessed and subsequently managed through a set of risk management processes, underpinned by a risk coordinator, to increase the likelihood of timely completion within anticipated budgets.

The Risk and Opportunity Management Process

Risk management, for this project team therefore, presented as an evolutionary and iterative process. Whilst the fundamental principles remain unaltered, de Coverley advised that in all instances the process itself should be tailored to fit the specific requirements and make-up of the individual projects within the programme. Risks and opportunities could be managed, however, through a tried-and-tested two phase approach early in the programme life cycle that generated a shared version of the truth that then would deliver a consistent and scale-able ongoing risk management process that was initially customer-driven and programme-owned. It was believed that Risk Action Plans designed to manage the risks identified were generally less costly if implemented earlier rather than later in the programme. The project team felt that it would manage its projects within this manner, illustrated graphically in the figure below.

Under my guidance, an initial set of risk workshops were conducted that identified risks and uncertainty to the projects. Through a variety of "brainstorming" and targeted discussions a "total" set of risks were identified against the following categories (representing a simplified project scope): Inbound Logistics (IL), Operations (OP), Marketing and Sales (MS), Human Resources (HR), Infrastructure (IF), Technologies (TE) and Outbound Logistics (OL). Market-leading risk software was, thereafter, utilised to undertake the actual generation of a risk model through a "monte carlo" simulation tool capable of simulating many thousands of iterations of the projects. The risks identified were created as tasks within a project schedule to enable the use of schedule and cost risks that were previously identified within the project team.

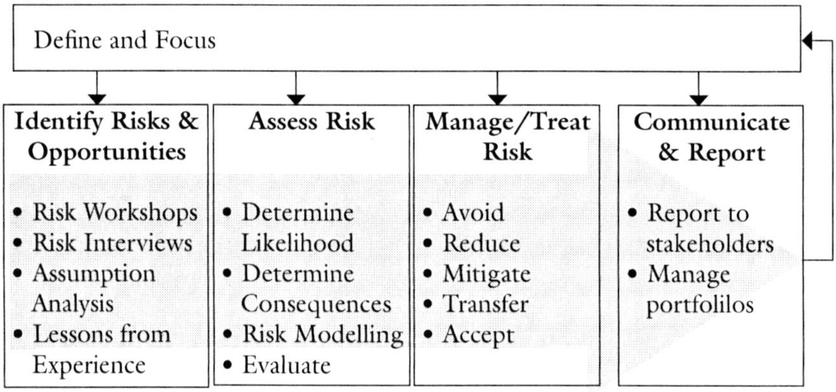

Outline Risk Management Methodology

A screen capture of the resulting risk model is shown in the following image:

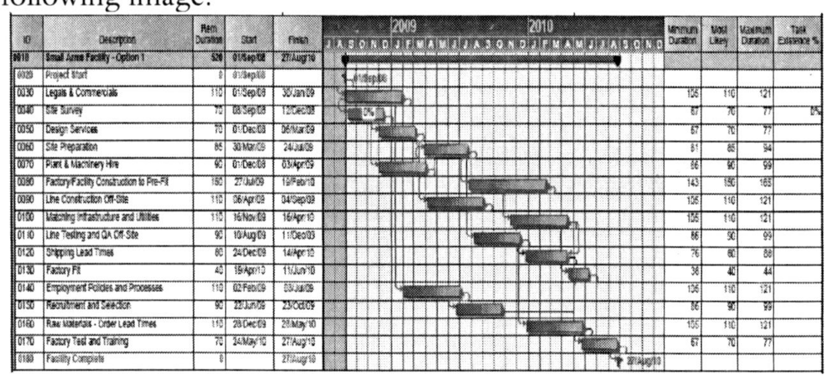

ID	Description	Rem Duration	Start	Finish	Minimum Duration	Most Likely	Maximum Duration	Task Existence %
0010	Small Arms Facility - Option 1	520	01/Sep/08	27/Aug/10				
0020	Project Start	0	01/Sep/08					
0030	Legals & Commercials	110	01/Sep/08	30/Jan/09	105	110	121	
0040	Site Survey	70	08/Sep/08	12/Dec/08	67	70	77	[illegible]
0050	Design Services	70	01/Dec/08	06/Mar/09	67	70	77	
0060	Site Preparation	85	30/Mar/09	24/Jul/09	81	85	94	
0070	Plant & Machinery Hire	90	01/Dec/08	03/Apr/09	86	90	99	
0080	Factory/Facility Construction to Pre-Fit	150	27/Jul/09	19/Feb/10	143	150	165	
0090	Line Construction Off-Site	110	06/Apr/09	04/Sep/09	105	110	121	
0100	Matching Infrastructure and Utilities	110	16/Nov/09	16/Apr/10	105	110	121	
0110	Line Testing and QA Off-Site	90	10/Aug/09	11/Dec/09	86	90	99	
0120	Shipping Lead Times	80	24/Dec/09	14/Apr/10	76	80	88	
0130	Factory Fit	40	19/Apr/10	11/Jun/10	38	40	44	
0140	Employment Policies and Processes	110	02/Feb/09	03/Jul/09	105	110	121	
0150	Recruitment and Selection	90	22/Jun/09	23/Oct/09	86	90	99	
0160	Raw Materials - Order Lead Times	110	28/Dec/09	28/May/10	105	110	121	
0170	Factory Test and Training	70	24/May/10	27/Aug/10	67	70	77	
0180	Facility Complete	0		27/Aug/10				

Risk Model Extract

The risk model could then generate histograms, such as that shown in the next figure, which demonstrated where risks resided in a project and suggested where management focus should be applied.

Wing Commander de Coverley explained that for each of the aircraft fleets for which the project team had a responsibility this risk management process would now be applied, generating valuable management information and informed management action.

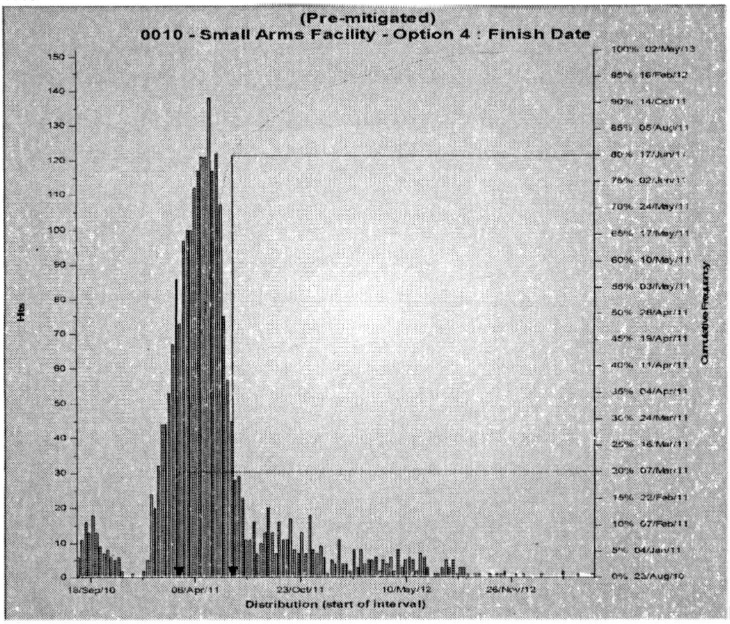

Risk Model Histogram

Wing Commander de Coverley became the self-described risk management "champion" within the project team. He was a military officer of almost thirty years' experience but was happy to subjugate himself to the power and insight of the management consultant, adopting the language and stance of the recently converted. Throughout the project team it was clear that de Coverley was widely respected and possessed of a fine military operational pedigree and record. Yet in the new (to the project team, at least) language of business consultancy he changed his military apparel for the consensual dress of managerialism, as offered by me as his consultant. He became a believer in the transformational power of risk management to any set of circumstances or condition, including those to be found within the military. This belief-system, like any corresponding act of religiosity, is projected across the population as a whole, in this case the EPCOT project team. As the organisation's Business Plan stated, following my engagement:

The project team will ensure that in running its business all areas will do so underpinned by risk and opportunity management, thereby ensuring best use of available resources. The risk and opportunity management process will ... utilise appropriate risk management tools.

A Cultural Refit

The importance placed by the team leadership in the art and science of risk management is worthy of a moment's reflection. Through the employment of consultants the UK military put in place processes and procedures to supposedly transfer notions of operational and financial risks to the industry base from the military front line. Indeed, this rationale and narrative of risk transfer formed part of the business logic for the defence change initiative launched in the UK, by management consultants, in 1997. Yet the business plan and team members of the project team I worked with did not articulate or discuss risk management as a process for transferring uncertainty and unknown costs and activities to industry, presumably through robust contractual mechanisms. Rather, for the EPCOT project team, management is management, intrinsically good and valuable, which can and should be applied to all aspects of the team's existence, certainly imported managerial constructs such as those associated with risk.

The transfer, from the project team to industry, of costs associated with identified individual risks does not feature, whether as proposition, practice or legitimisation. There is, simply, a set of directed activities and tool kits through which the project team can practise management. The practice itself is an objective, even end-state, in its own right.

This analysis suggests to me that the purpose of management consultancy, through these sorts of engagements, was actually to dilute the military; if you like, to wean it from a taxonomy of conflict and military service to one of business and a language of management. Inserting a risk management process had no discernible benefit other than to reinforce this sense of managerial triumph over traditional military values. The consultant became the high priest of managerialism, but the practice itself was already hollow and tainted. Also, my fees for this effort were in the tens of thousands of dollars, borne by the taxpayer. As this was but one project team of many, I estimate that the cost of consultancy services to the UK Ministry of Defence for risk management services would have been about $5 million dollars per annum between 1997 and today. Only the most generous of observers could describe this as value for money, or even sensible management. Indeed, almost immediately following my disengagement from the EPCOT project team, the practices of risk management I championed, and they paid hard currency for, were discontinued. So much for the enduring benefits of consultancy.

Forget Risk, Remember Management

Through this vignette of management consultancy there seems to be an enduring belief in the principles of management that clients are keen to pay for. But in pursuing this agenda the project team was prepared to abandon its military culture which, on the face of it, had endured for an epoch, and replace it with loose-fitting general business managerialism—as articulated through risk and opportunity management. It seems clear to me now that organisations in business or government should embrace and protect their core cultures as, somehow, transcending the management fashions of the day. Perhaps this is a point we can reflect upon as we turn our eyes to management practices around programme and project management and recovery.

Notes

1. I first write about this team in John Louth, *A Low Dishonest Decade: Smart Acquisition and Defence Procurement into the New Millennium* (Cardiff: UWIC, 2010).
2. See Rory Burke, *Project Management: Planning and Control Techniques* (London: John Wiley & Sons, 2003), pp. 252-53.

6. Programme and Project Management and Recovery

Recovering Programmes and Projects

The next principal consulting area I was involved in during my time as a consultant was the design and delivery of complex programmes or projects, their associated control mechanisms and governance, and the recovery of existing programmes that had started to, somehow, steam off the rails. Things that go wrong are a rich seam for management consultants to mine. It invariably starts in despair and desperation—the client's! Within my practice, my senior directors and sales teams always relished the call from an existing or potential client who said he or she had troubles with their business or activity and were lost for a response. The appropriate response for the companies I worked for was always to sell an "improvement programme" or "recovery programme" which worked well on a set of PowerPoint slides during the sale to the client but was always much more difficult to deliver on the ground. But then, or course, life is more nuanced, rich and complicated than our management models will allow.

The practices of portfolio, programme and project management are phenomena of modern modes of management. In terms of the overall genre, a portfolio is a number of unrelated programmes and possibly projects that are being run by a single project management entity. In contrast, a programme is a large, usually capital, project that may be subdivided into a number of smaller, though significant, projects to achieve a single, common programme goal. A project, on the other hand, is a temporary, though formal, endeavour to create a unique product or service through a singular scope of work and specification. In many ways the differences in definition and emphasis is just a question of scale and the subjective analysis of the professional or consultant in question. For me, portfolio, programme and project concepts are highly fluid and contingent, changing from sector to sector.

The Body of Knowledge

There is a huge and self-referencing body of knowledge relating to project management that can be found in the works of professional bodies such as the Project Management Institute in the USA or the Association of Project Managers in the UK. In addition there is the International Association of Project Managers and the Australian Institute of Project Managers. All of these institutions produce standards and guidelines framed as best practice and there are independent quality standards such as the UK's ISO 10006 to legitimise the practices of project management. To run activities as projects, utilising the benefits of this supposed body of knowledge, provides rich pickings for the management consulting profession.

When a management or organisational activity is established as a specific, named project, such as the reorganisation of a set of businesses processes, the consultant is able to generate a work structure that intersects the needs of the project, the organisation, a range of internal and external stakeholders and individual team members. He or she is able to do this through the introduction of activities and artefacts always associated with a project. For example, a schedule of work is raised, with a recognisable and clear beginning and end date, and end-state, come to that, where the outputs and benefits of the project are overtly captured and articulated. There will be a life cycle to the project within this start and finish timeline, decanted into a number of distinct phases or project sub-activities. These activities are usually unique to that particular schedule of work, and non-repetitive. Resources are aligned to these activities along with the roles and responsibilities of team members. A single point of responsibility for each activity or suite of activities is stated, which allows authority to be delegated from the project manager throughout the work space. Finally, this division of labour and scheduling is captured within a project budget.

The benefits of using a project management approach are said to flow from the needs of the project itself, so that the project manager or consultant is charged with developing a plan through which the project can be compared and controlled thus assuring that the project meets its predetermined objectives or outputs. To do this, timely and accurate management information is required from a pre-positioned project planning and control system matched to the scope of work and schedule of activities. This is usually achieved by structuring controls around a work breakdown structure for project reporting and an organisational breakdown structure for broader corporate reporting.

If an activity requires a project, therefore—and modern management seems capable of turning any traditional business activity into a project—then project management expertise is usually required to plan for, establish and embed this innovation. Consequently, there are myriad management consultancies that have established themselves as project management experts. Indeed, I worked for such a business at the beginning of the century selling project management reform solutions to governments and industry. Sensible, reflective management was merely re-packaged into the language of the programme and project, and sold at a good margin to the client in question.

Circularity of Consulting Offerings

In a beautiful example of circularity of thinking, the discipline of project management is heavily laced with change management components as the former is often described as the most efficient and effective way of introducing change or improvements to an organisation, defining what needs to be achieved in terms of performance, time, cost and risk to the project. Indeed, through the introduction of the latter term "risk," project management also embraces the phenomenon of risk management, allowing the skilled consultant to introduce to an engagement the full lexicon of language at his disposal; change, project management, risk and reform.

Most Americans I have worked with over the years would describe project management as possessing nine characteristics. These knowledge areas are championed by the US Project Management Institute:

- Project Integration—which brings together planning, execution and control of an activity;
- Project Scope—which involves accepting (or, of course, rejecting) activities into a project;
- Time Management—an activity that includes sequencing of work, estimating and the overall management of the schedule;
- Cost Management—a set of activities bringing together budgeting and cost controls;
- Quality Management—which involves quality planning, conditioning, testing, evaluating and the assurance function;
- Project Human Resources Management—the processes to ensure the greatest benefit is received from people involved in the project;
- Communication—which involves the collection and dissemination of project management information to a wide range of stakeholders;
- Risk Management—the process for identifying, estimating, analysing and responding to project risks and uncertainties;

- Procurement—which bring together the processes for acquiring goods, services and know-how to a project.

All of these distinct activities combined can make for a very large and escalating consulting engagement that spans analysis, planning and delivery functions. The potential for the consultant to cross-sell is enormous and a frequent consequence of project management. Indeed, a senior colleague from an advisory business I worked in stated that we specialised in project management consultancy simply because of the opportunities for follow-on work the designation allowed. No wonder consultants love project management—you can almost write your own cheque.

Recovering an Aircraft Project

The UK Ministry of Defence had trouble with the project management of the supply chain of a particularly elderly and fragile aircraft type that was being used by the Royal Air Force (RAF). My company was contracted to diagnose the problem and advise on a solution, a task that fell to me and a small team of consultants that I formed. Using a form of risk management techniques outlined above, we were able to identify the tensions within the supply chain as related to the programme of activities relating to this aircraft from its current operations to its out-of-service date. All of the information we used was gleaned from the RAF project team and was readily available to them prior to our engagement. Where we added value was in organising this information systematically against the forward schedule for the aircraft. Having done this, it was clear that the next stage was to actually visit the key suppliers to validate the information we were holding to assess whether recommendations were robust or not. This was not a simple task as the key suppliers were located in North America and the Middle East, whilst the RAF project team was based in the east of the United Kingdom and the aircraft themselves were based and operated from southern England.

A visit schedule was arranged for myself and a colleague starting with companies in Canada, going on to the United States and then on to Jordan and the United Arab Emirates. It was an eye-opening set of visits. On arriving in Canada to review the first business significant within the supply chain to the aircraft it became abundantly clear that very few people from the project team in Britain had ever visited this key supplier, let alone knew of the ownership and governance arrangements being applied to the business. A key financier to the company had flown in from his tax haven in the Caribbean and whilst he appeared a decent man properly concerned with his investment we deduced that the financial health of the business was relying heavily on the disposition of one elderly gentlemen of substantial, though finite, means. And this was a sole supplier to a Royal Air Force major capability, one critical to the defence and national security of the UK. It wasn't so much that the logistics programme for the aircraft was overheated and problematic with pinch-points, as originally proposed by the client and initially diagnosed by us, there were critical vulnerabilities associated with the corporate health of sole suppliers that could ground the aircraft. This was discovered not by smart consulting models and analysis but by visiting the supplier, observing and reflecting on what had been seen. This could, and should, have been achieved by the client through a programme of regular visits and engagements, and if the money that had been spent on consultants had been committed to a travelling budget I am confident that the need for engaging the consultants would not have arisen.

But it does not end there. The company we were visiting was staffed by good people who worked hard and did their best but, again, by observing and reflecting it became obvious that much of the items being sold to the RAF as consumable parts for the aircraft were being stored and maintained in a highly unconventional manner. One day a colleague and I asked to see the storage facility for parts that were being despatched to the United Kingdom for almost immediate use on the aircraft. We were taken into the country to view an ex-chicken farm where, amongst the straw and chicken runs, were stored myriad engine, gearbox and airframe parts, most certified for use—not by an engineer, but by the owner of the business. I am no engineer myself, but I would think that members of the RAF and the British taxpayer would not consider it appropriate for aircraft parts to be stored and certified in this manner. But it was not a consulting skill that identified this of course, rather just the ability—and commitment—to visit, view and think.

Continuing this theme, on visits to businesses in the United States we were told that certain suppliers were exiting the market as a deliberate corporate strategy, in response to a principal business from the sector seeking to hold a monopoly on contracts to the Royal Air Force. This response was actually causing the supplier market to congeal and contract, driving up component prices and increasing lead-times for securing parts to the RAF. Relatively minor adjustments to the Service's procurement strategy—by avoiding single-source contracts, for example—could have greatly eased this trend thereby countering the risk of the aircraft being grounded. But this could only be deduced by visiting the suppliers and seeking to understand their concerns. As one of the more junior consultants confided at the time, the client did not need consulting skills to help him deliver his responsibilities, just basic observational skills. These he possessed in droves; they had simply been misplaced as the client clung to his comfort blanket of consultancy.

Third Party Reviews

Of course, it is often desirable for a third party, such as a consultant, to review a business or a relationship to check on its health and vitality, especially one configured as a programme or project subject to the project manager's body of knowledge as reviewed above. Indeed such an argument is often made for the perceived benefits of a consulting engagement, and my client certainly found our activities highly useful and was happy to pay for the work. But the real point is that the money belonged to the taxpayers of the United Kingdom and the skills utilised—observation, reflection, communication—were straightforward management competencies already possessed by the client. We were doing work, perhaps even important work, that should have been routine for the client. But because it was wrapped in the sophisticated lexicon of consultancy it was perceived as specialised, complicated, valuable and, of course, expensive. It is not a stretch to suggest that such a mindset contributes overtly to notions of national budget deficits, fiscal constraints and public sector financial crises, all of which feature heavily in Western life following the collapse of the international financial system in 2008.

Management consultants are making good profits through the lenses of programme and project management and recovery, perhaps aligned to notions of risk management and organisational transformation. However, the real cash-cow is the practice of strategy consulting, to which we now turn, as strategy can open up the need for better project management, the insertion of a risk and opportunity management system or a transformation project. The potential for cross-selling is almost limitless with strategy engagements. As we move to this subject I would ask the reader to keep in mind the tension between what is specialised, bespoke to the consultant, rare and valuable, and what is better conceptualised as common sense.

7. Strategy Consulting

The Practice of Strategy

The practice of strategy is often an illusive and illusory concept, but one which the consulting professionals take very seriously and earn substantial revenues from. As we have seen above, the consultants of McKinsey & Co., for example, regard themselves and are regarded by others as a major strategy house, deriving strategic choices and supporting the implementation of strategic change to myriad government and corporate clients.[1] But just what do we mean by strategy? I shall try and answer this by addressing an event that many would describe as strategically significant.

Strategic Corporate Merger—A Case-Study

The collapsed proposed merger of BAE Systems with EADS in 2012 generated much coverage and debate right across the defence communities in the United Kingdom, Europe, North America and beyond, with a great deal of passion spent on all sides of the argument. One of the reasons, of course, for this seemingly dramatic response is that the proposition was so unexpected. On September 12, the boards of both EADS and BAE Systems stunned the market, and a number of governments, with a nil-premium merger plan whereby Europe's largest civil aerospace business, EADS, would join forces with Europe's (and Britain's) largest defence design, manufacturing, maintenance and service corporation. The combination would create a European version of the US giant Boeing, with a balanced pan-market portfolio of military and commercial aerospace interests and products.

Under the terms of the proposal the new combined group would be sixty per cent owned by EADS shareholders with the balance held by investors in BAE Systems. The market capitation of the entity, post transaction, would be in the region of £30 billion with annual sales of almost twice that value. It would have 220,000 employees worldwide and undoubtedly would dwarf in turnover both Boeing and Lockheed Martin.[2] Of note, the aerospace element of the new business would probably be listed in Holland whilst the defence division would be registered in the United Kingdom.[3]

A main element of the commentary and analysis revolved around the strategic implications of the proposed combination, with some politicians in the UK talking about the need to understand the *strategic case* for change in the first place and the *strategic consequences* of the transaction's failure.[4] If "strategy" was important to the success, or otherwise, of the transaction and how it should be analysed, the least that could be expected of commentators, politicians, officials and industrialists is clarity around what is meant by this concept. Strategy, though, proves illusive and illusionary to many charged with its exercise.

For example, in May 2011, I attended a dinner to celebrate the efforts of those committed to British defence and national security.[5] Present were the then Secretary of State for Defence, Service Chiefs and senior officers from the three armed forces, and leading figures from industry and commerce. During the main course a conversation unfolded concerned with strategy in the context of the United Kingdom. It became apparent that some contributors were talking about national strategy, one or two about military strategy and the remaining participants offered thoughts and perspectives on corporate strategies. The conversation flowed as if these three concepts of strategy were one and the same phenomenon, with words and phrases used interchangeably. Yet, intuitively, state strategy in the contemporary world would appear to be different from notions of a company's corporate strategy, with military strategy—what?—an extension or subset of state intent on the battlefield. The question was: how to make sense of a "narrative of strategy" that seemed to offer explanations of all things to all people, pretty much all of the time.

During this period, as I sought to understand more about this omnipotent sense of strategy through semi-structured interviews and informal conversations with industrialists, military leaders, officials and politicians, one constant message seemed to be repeated. Just as individuals often conceive of themselves as great drivers and wonderful lovers, so people of the defence community in the United Kingdom sensed that they were all really good strategists and that notions of strategy were important to their work, irrespective of whether that work was undertaken in military uniform, directing activities in a factory or in Whitehall or Westminster. "Strategy," "strategic coherence" and "strategic awareness" were pivotal, oft-repeated, defence concepts, with many hours, a good deal of money and great efforts consumed in these practices of strategy. What seemed to be missing though, at least through the perspective of interviews and conversations undertaken, was clarity of purpose, unambiguous meaning and total differentiation between concepts of corporate strategy, military strategy and national strategy. This matters enormously, especially in the debate around the merits or otherwise of corporate tie-ups such as BAE Systems' proposed merger with EADS, when the public narrative revolves around what action should be taken in the national strategic interest.

Moreover, during the course of writing this book, the UK's Public Administration Select Committee published a report identifying a lack of strategic coherence in the United Kingdom.[6] Policymakers and stakeholders across defence, the Select Committee commented, were adept at a managerialist language of strategy but not at its practice, with government woefully inadequate in articulating or choreographing the delivery of national priorities and objectives. The Report went on to state that:[7]

> In general, strategic thinking is not highly prized in the UK. This stems from our culture: we privilege empirical evidence and empiricism in the philosophical underpinnings of decision-making. This has worked for us in many ways for a long time but this clearly is inadequate in a world where the interconnections, influences and politics of other countries are so very strong. The UK thus must develop the capability to think and act strategically from the top of the Executive down through parliament, media, academia, civil society, schools, pressure groups, industry bodies and individuals.

There is, consequently, something both worthwhile and timely in exploring the intersection of concepts of strategy and national security. I proceed as follows: a short discussion of strategy as national imperative follows which is, subsequently, tested against ideas of corporate strategy and strategic choice. The narrative is anchored in a consideration of the hard realities facing the executives of BAE Systems, as a timely reflection of why the subject of strategy is more than just an academic pursuit.

Strategy—A Simple Concept?

There is little doubt that the concept of strategy is having a resurgence, especially as affordability, efficiency and economy drive decision-making post the financial collapse of 2008. A wide range of articles have peppered the RUSI Journal and other publications in recent times, and Gwyn Prins' excellent occasional paper of October 2011 successfully explores the very British way of "doing" strategy.[8] It would be both repetitive and unproductive to replay those arguments and insights here. Rather, for this author, strategy in the context of defence and national security can be conceptualised as a relatively straightforward idea. In terms of planning, resourcing and execution the levels of strategy are the grand strategic, the military strategic, the operational and the tactical, as found at the very heart of British defence doctrine for many years.[9] In this context, grand strategy is the application of national resources and know-how to achieve national policy objectives in the most efficient and economic manner. Its purpose, consequently, is to direct and provide coherence to all aspects of national policy and execution, and resides at the political strategic level of government. Grand strategy draws lessons from the past but is forward looking to anticipate tomorrow's hazards, risks and opportunities, so that Gwyn Prins is right to assert that its essential condition is to bring "ways and means" into correct alignment with "ends."[10]

Military strategy, not surprisingly, should be simply viewed as the manner and method of applying military resources to the time-bound achievement of grand strategic objectives. In other words, it is the military component of grand strategy and should be formulated and exercised once the political direction is set. At an operational level within the military, commanders are concerned with the direction and application of military resources to achieve military strategic objectives. Likewise, the tactical level involves the direction of military resources and know-how to meet operational objectives. So strategy, it would appear, is not an overly complicated concept when applied to notions of defence or national security. Indeed, strategy as an articulation of defence doctrine appears well covered and reasonably well understood. Rather, the difficulties occur when defence businesses are added to the brew.

A private sector company's concept of "ends," "ways" and "means" is usually much more complicated and nuanced than the simple narrative explanation of "grand strategy" and its components outlined above. This becomes especially significant when the private sector forms such an essential element of the overall defence effort. In the United Kingdom, over forty per cent of the defence budget is spent within the private sector.[11] Moreover, in 2010 for example, the United Kingdom deployed over 7,000 private sector contractors to directly support military operations overseas, in Afghanistan, the Gulf, Balkan states and across the Indian Ocean. Contractor support to operations in this year consumed over £2.6 billion or, in budgetary terms, close to forty-five per cent of the total overseas military effort.[12] It is clear that the corporate strategies of these defence businesses matter as the companies form such a large constituent part of the modern defence and national security effort.

Corporate Strategy

Corporate strategy is different from national or grand strategy and the two concepts should not be treated as elements of the same indivisible phenomenon. In business, the study of strategy and the foundations of strategic thinking can be traced to a number of influential thinkers and propositions that became prominent in the years immediately following the end of the Second World War. For example, Peter Drucker, writing in 1946, looked at businesses operating in the United States such as General Motors, IBM and Sears Roebuck, and concluded that the most successful companies combined centralised planning and goal-setting functions, and that culturally they were essentially outward looking in focus.[13] Business strategy, therefore, was primarily about identifying customers, understanding their needs and purchasing power and satisfying customer ambitions in a profitable manner.

Thinkers such as Theodore Levitt and Igor Ansoff[14] published broad perspectives on corporate strategy as blueprints for expansion planning, competitor assessments, market scanning and resource allocation. Management consultancies such as McKinsey and the Boston Consulting Group (BCG) became strategy houses blending market analyses and research with microeconomic financial theory to produce complex, compelling and in-demand strategic perspectives on competitors, costs and customers. Boards of directors could use such strategic thinking to conceptualise the business world, plan responses and implement those plans, testing results against the earlier developed corporate explanatory model.

It sounds quite straightforward in principle, but the challenges begin to feature when it is realised that the academic and practitioner literature on strategic management in business is vast and contradictory—it could hardly be otherwise as so many consulting companies and academics have made such a good living over the years promoting their own specific approach to corporate strategy.[15] Rather, understanding the use of the word "strategy" in business—especially defence businesses, as with this example—becomes much more multidimensional and fragile.

For instance, there is a clear difference in perspectives on the organisation and its particular strategic choice, depending upon whether the stakeholder is a shareholder, manager, employee, customer or somebody holding a wider interest. In the context of the potential deal between BAE Systems and EADS, understanding BAE Systems' strategic interest is not without problems. For the shareholder it is very much around maximising shareholder value. The directors and senior leaders, whilst legally charged with pursuing the shareholders' interests, understandably put a premium on growth, hence management's championing of the proposed merger. The customer probably wishes for stability and for the business to be a viable going concern, whilst the employee, no doubt, amongst other things, simply wishes to know that his or her job is secure for the long term. So that a corporation like BAE Systems long-term interest is not an uncontested phenomenon.

Of course, most business schools in the developed world will have a definition of strategy. It will usually say something like, "a company's top management plan to attain outcomes consistent with the organisation's mission, ambition and goals."[16] But the realities of managing a complicated business suggest that strategy—as both a corporate roadmap and articulation of the day-to-day endeavours of delivery—is much more complicated than this simple definition allows.[17] Rather, it makes more sense to conceive of corporate strategy as a *plan*, a *pattern*, a *position*, a *perspective* and even a *ploy*. The notion of a plan is self-evident, as that of a guide or course of action from today to tomorrow. Strategy as a pattern is equally clear. A company that manufactures and markets high-quality, expensive merchandise over many years has a pattern of following a high-end strategy and is understood by customers, competitors and employees in this context. Strategy is also a position, namely matching products and services to markets. It is also a perspective, a company's particular way of operating, its culture and values. But it can also be a ploy; for example, the practice of buying large swathes of land may convince competitors and other stakeholders that the company is seeking to expand. The real strategic purpose may be more cynical, that being to prevent a competitor's expansion whilst keeping value on the Balance Sheet.

So, strategy is not simply about matching activities to long-term goals. For companies, it is much more concerned with a complexity of choices around a number of competing forces and perspectives. This makes it difficult and inappropriate to place corporate strategy in the lexicon of national or grand strategy. They are different concepts and practices. BAE System's quest for a merger with EADS has to be viewed through this prism if it is to be properly understood.

The Strategic Choice

Consequently the corporate ambition for the merger cannot and should not be seen through the explanatory lens of UK national strategy even though it would have impacted upon Britain's principal defence and national security contractor. Much more prescient is to try and understand the corporate strategic choices open to the board of BAE Systems and, in this context, why a tie-up with a European aerospace manufacturer seemed so alluring. Also, whilst it is too simplistic to argue that corporate strategy is somehow taking precedence over national strategy, what seems significant from events so far is that the British strategic interest is being framed and influenced by BAE System's corporate imperative. To the extent, perhaps, that an argument could be made that British national strategy, in part, is the sum of disparate, and changeable, corporate strategies.

Acknowledging that stakeholders and commentators conceive multiple scenarios for the future of BAE Systems, if it is accepted that defence budgets in the West will reduce in real terms over the rest of the decade,[18] the company probably has a minimum of four distinct, though not necessarily mutually exclusive, options.

First, it could acknowledge and embrace this probable reduction in revenues and manage decline as effectively as possible. This would probably involve regular redundancy programmes and restrictions on recruitment and development spending as revenues declined and new orders reduced. Second, the company could seek to access a new market—civilian vehicles, for instance—through purchase, to balance or counterweight the intended retrenchment in defence spending by governments. Third, it could consider a total strategic exit from defence in the mid-term (or split the business on geographical lines), either by returning monies to investors and other providers of finance or investing in parallel industries such as commercial shipbuilding or freight distribution. Fourth, directors could seek to consolidate and merge, searching for growth through volume and the strength of a much broader balance sheet. There are no other smart ideas and, realistically, either accepting stagnation followed by corporate decline or exiting defence en masse are just not realistic options. Buying a non-defence business to enable diversification seems a somewhat tired and tame option hardly likely to be applauded by the markets, so the company is left with a single, bold choice almost by default.[19]

Naturally, the merits, or otherwise, of the proposed transaction could only be judged on the detail. At the time of writing precious little of that is still to find its way into the public domain. It is well known that concerns existed in governments in Europe and the United States around notions of sovereignty, the need to protect national intellectual property (especially in the United States), the case for or against European defence industrial integration and the possibility of further redundancies. Weighed against these very real concerns was the opportunity to create a European monolith of real bulk, with the confidence of a robust order book, a strong balance sheet and an extensive list of government and civil clients. It was a finely balanced argument, of course, but understanding what other strategic options exist for BAE Systems is equally challenging. Whatever happens over the next months and years as the consequences of the failed merger are debated, the "do nothing" option for BAE Systems, probably, can now be discounted. Which means that corporate strategy will be driving, of necessity, United Kingdom national strategy, at least as it relates to the defence industrial element of the military instrument. Any discussion on strategy has to recognise and take account of this interdependency and dynamic.

There is, therefore, a danger that ideas around strategy smash into a homogenised mash, as was the case at the defence dinner I attended in 2011 which was referred to at the beginning of this chapter. The realisation that this "mash" had contributors from the political, industrial and military elite of the United Kingdom and its allies only adds to this concern. Rather, national or grand strategy, as it is often called, is different from corporate strategy, and whilst military strategy can legitimately be seen as an expression of the former, corporate strategy as a phenomenon in the private sector is too complex and subtle to be seen ever as an articulation of national ambition.

This is significant when an important event occurs such as the proposed merger between BAE Systems, Britain's largest defence contractor, and EADS, the aerospace giant registered in Europe. Much of the political debate and commentary has revolved around notions of the UK national strategic interest and what would be best for that country, with barely an acknowledgement that BAE Systems has a responsibility to pursue its best and most appropriate corporate strategy even if this were to somehow diverge from national, governmental preferences. The interests of other important stakeholders, especially the shareholders, seem to be relegated in the coverage as the perceived dominance of the search for the national interest strives to take hold. This occurs, partly, because of this confused narrative of strategy within the United Kingdom.

Indeed, it has been consistently argued by the chair of the Public Administration Select Committee[20] that government does not have an articulated national strategy and that both Number 10 and the Cabinet Office act as coordination cells rather than offering cogent strategic direction. What I am suggesting is that, whether or not government does "grand strategy," the very language of strategy as a subject itself is confused and often misrepresented. Policymakers, industrialists and commanders can only effectively manage what they can conceptualise and define. Much more care needs to be taken as the debate on British strategy-making continues. For continue it must, as neither the House Of Commons Public Administration Select Committee nor the Defence Select Committee believe that Britain possesses a robust, sensible or properly defined national security strategy.[21]

> Neither committee thinks that the problem can be fixed by marginal adjustment. They believe that the international departments of state have poor maps and compasses with which to plot their detailed courses and dispositions.

Poor decision-making, questionable analysis and exaggerated, shrill commentaries inevitably follow as a consequence of a confused and broken narrative of strategy. When tough national and corporate decisions are needed in the face of profound global hazards, geopolitical uncertainties and fiscal constraints, this lack of definitive coherence and rigour may prove collectively and continually debilitating.

So, strategy is both confused and, somehow, profoundly important to both businesses and nation-states. How can consultants, as a consequence, simply seek to offer strategy services to clients given this inherent complexity, confusion and significance? It is a good question, but a significant proportion of the consulting profession resides in the strategy space, seeking to develop "new" strategies for their client base at significant cost.

When I was charged with advising on strategic options to my companies' clients I always started from a premise of certainty. The quest for the "right" strategy was to be linear and causal in nature, highly rational, deterministic and objective. Such confidence usually made the sale. The world though, as illustrated above, for companies and countries alike, is much more complicated, fragile and uncertain than my glib promises would ever allow. We need to remember this when we both seek to identify a strategy, and most definitely when we are preparing to pay a third party huge sums to help us with this quest.

Notes

1. For example, see McKinsey, *Strength to Innovate* (London: McKinsey & Co., 1991), *Efficiency and Effectiveness: A Guide* (London: McKinsey & Co., 2003) and *McKinsey on Government* (London: McKinsey & Co., 2013).
2. For Financial Year 2011, Boeing made sales of £43 billion whilst Lockheed Martin's group turnover was in the region of £29 billion, as reported by Karl West, "Trident Threat to BAE Deal," *Sunday Times*, September 14, 2012.
3. Private interview with a senior UK industrialist, conducted by the author on September 17, 2012.
4. As an example, this was discussed in the debate between Lord Reid, Ben Wallace MP and the author on the BBC Today programme on September 14, 2012. See also, James Boxell and Anousha Sakoui, "Big Questions Surrounding Defence Tie-up," in *Financial Times*, Friday, September 21, 2012; David Gelles and

Ed Crooks, "US Defence Groups Reassess Strategies," in *Financial Times*, Wednesday, September 19, 2012.

5. London Chamber of Commerce Defence Dinner 2011, held at the Imperial War Museum, London on June 7, 2011.
6. House of Commons Public Administration Select Committee, *Strategic Thinking in Government: without national strategy, can viable government strategy emerge?* (London: The Stationery Office, 2012). See also House of Commons Public Administration Select Committee, *Who Does UK National Strategy?* (London: The Stationery Office, 2010).
7. House of Commons Public Administration Select Committee, *Strategic Thinking in Government: without national strategy, can viable government strategy emerge?* Volume II (London: The Stationery Office, 2012) Ev. w14.
8. See Gwyn Prins, *The British Way of Strategy-Making: Vital Lessons for Our Times* (London: RUSI Occasional Paper, 2011). See also Peter Layton, "The Idea of Grand Strategy," *RUSI Journal* (vol. 157, no. 4, August/September 2012), pp. 56-61. See also Lukas Milevski, "A Collective Failure of Grand Strategy: The West's Unintended Wars of Choice," *RUSI Journal* (vol. 156, no. 1, February/March 2011) pp. 30-33. See also Matthew Savill, "UK Security Strategy: Clarity or Compromise?" *Defence Studies* (vol. 11, no. 3, September 2011), pp. 359-95.
9. See, for example, Ministry of Defence Joint Warfare Publication (JWP) 0.01 *British Defence Doctrine* (London: MoD CS(M)G, 1996). See also John Baylis, James Wirtz, Colin S. Gray and Eliot Cohen, *Strategy in the Contemporary World* (Oxford: OUP, 2007).
10. Gwyn Prins, op. cit., p. 17.
11. See Henrik Heidenkamp, John Louth and Trevor Taylor, *The Defence Industrial Ecosystem: Delivering Security in an Uncertain World* (London: RUSI, 2011), p. 7.
12. See Henrik Heidenkamp, *Sustaining the UK's Defence Effort: Contractor Support to Operations Market Dynamics* (London: RUSI, 2012).
13. See Peter Drucker, *Concepts of the Corporation* (Boston: MIT, 1946). A useful summary of Peter Drucker's contribution can be found in Richard Koch's *Strategy* (London: Prentice Hall, 2000). Also see Henry Mintzberg, Bruce Ahlstrand and Joseph Lampel, *Strategy Safari: A Guided Tour Through the Wilds of Strategic Management* (New York: The Free Press, 1998). Furthermore, a very useful summary of strategy writers appears in Part 2 of the Koch book.
14. See T. Levitt, "Marketing Myopia" in *Harvard Business Review* (July-August 1960) pp. 45-56. See also H. I. Ansoff, *Corporate Strategy* (New York: McGraw-Hill, 1965).
15. Between 1995 and 2000, for example, the global demand for strategy management consultants grew from $51 billion to $114 billion. See Sugata Biswas and Daryl Twitchell, *Management Consulting: A Complete Guide to the Industry* (New York: John Wiley & Sons, 2002) p. 7.

16. See P. Wright, C. Pringle and M. Kroll, *Strategic Management Text and Cases* (Needham Heights: Allyn & Bacon, 1992).
17. Private author interview with defence industrialist on November 19, 2011 in London. Additional private interviews with investors and fund managers on September 18, 2012.
18. See Malcolm Chalmers, "The Lean Years: Defence Consequences of the Fiscal Crisis," in Michael Codner and Michael Clarke (eds.), *A Question of Security: The British Defence Review in an Age of Austerity* (London: I.B. Tauris, 2011), pp. 33-75.
19. See Ian King, "This Time BAE Has No Plan B," in *The Times*, September 25, 2012.
20. The Hon Bernard Jenkin MP. See House of Commons Public Administration Select Committee, *Strategic Thinking in Government: without national strategy, can viable government strategy emerge?* (London: The Stationery Office, 2012). See also House of Commons Public Administration Select Committee, *Who Does UK National Strategy?* (London: The Stationery Office, 2010). See also, Bernard Jenkin and George Grant, *The Tipping Point: British National Strategy and the UK's Future World Role* (London: The Henry Jackson Society, 2011).
21. Gwyn Prins, op. cit., p. 1. There is, of course, the key document, HM Government, A Strong Britain in an Age of Uncertainty: The National Security Strategy, Cm 7953 (London: The Stationery office, 2010). Prins' argument is that, despite the title, this document in neither strategic in scope nor effectively articulates United Kingdom national or grand strategy.

SECTION THREE

8. Consultancy as Common Sense—The Practice of Management Consultancy

Here to Stay

The practice of management consultancy is here to stay and there is little doubt that smart people with a variety of experiences and qualifications employed judiciously on a temporary basis can be a great help to clients. But as both the examples and broader discussion indicate above, its practice resides in common sense and the use of sensible and reflective management and people skills rather than some professional consultant-only competence set that takes years to develop and hone, such as the skills of an architect, an engineer or a dentist. In this section I deconstruct the key skills of a successful consultant, framing consultancy as the application of common sense and managerial knowledge rather than the product of a unique, bounded and differentiated profession.

Most professional consultants, or consultants writing books about their subject, usually talk about consulting principles. As we have discussed, quite often consulting will be framed around the need to fundamentally generate change; that is the practice of helping one person, organisation, government department or other form of relationship move from one performance state to another. This requires a consulting "change model" to be applied to the client's requirement so that the basic steps of consultancy are common to each engagement. As a consequence, therefore, the practice of consultancy is the practice of applying this change model, tailored for the scale, context and demands of the particular assignment in question. To understand consultancy we need to appreciate this change model.

Mick Cope is a successful business writer and consultant.[1] He has written and lectured extensively on management consulting and his change model is framed around seven simple steps, what he describes as the "Seven Cs." The stages, when combined, form a complete framework for consultancy and are similar to many other practitioner guides on the subject. Before working-through the Seven Cs it is worth pointing out that many consultants find such a guide invaluable, and I have been told by a number of consultants that Mick Cope's framework has a high utility within the profession.

The first C is the "client" whereby the consultant has to orientate him or herself to see the world through the client's eyes, to understand the problem as perceived by the person signing the cheques. The second C is "clarify," a process through which the consultant checks with the client the nature of the change sought, who is to be included and what the risks or uncertainties might be. "Create" is the third C where the consultant develops a plan for implementation to deliver the required outcomes articulated by the earlier stages. The fourth C is "change" itself—inevitably—a process of discovery by the consultant and client of what drives and underscores the engagement's change process. "Confirm," the fifth C, allows the consultant to demonstrate and ensure that the required change has actually occurred, whilst the sixth C, "continue" encourages the sharing of knowledge and skills between client and consultant. The final stage "close" suggests that the consultant disengages from the client with flair and alacrity, identifying in the process future business opportunities for the consultant's firm to undertake.

This is a useful model and if it helps consultants perform their roles it seems churlish to be critical. But it has always seemed to me that such models emphasise and stress matters that should be common sense and just good business. Assuming that there is a performance problem, the company in question requires a period of diagnoses, some form of agreement on the nature of the problem, an executable, time-bound plan to put it right, management activity to implement the plan and a way of measuring the success, or otherwise, of the outcomes. This is the stuff of management and should not require a consulting engagement or change model to enact. It asks questions, not of the quality of the consultant, but of the knowledge and ability of the client.

If we accept the efficacy and presence of the common consulting practice of a change model framework, the skills associated with these seven stages is relatively easy to capture and understand. The ability to negotiate is especially useful in engaging with a new client and is emphasised, perhaps, at the "client" stage of the model. Coaching and business development are skills useful at the "continue" and "close" stages of the model, whilst facilitating and influencing are pivotal right across the seven stages. Analytical skills and data gathering are also useful across the spectrum of activities, but perhaps especially at the "clarify" stage.

These skills and competencies, of course, echo those picked at in Chapter 3. The interesting thing for me is that the combination of negotiating, coaching, influencing and strong analytics are precisely the combination of skills and preferences that I have seen throughout my career possessed by the most successful business development directors and sales professionals. The confluence between consultancy and sales, once more, raises its head, so that management consultancy, amongst other explanations, could be the transformation of the common-sense practice of business into commodified, homogenised product.

This seems a significant critique of the practice of consulting. At one level of analysis, as seen through a self-referencing change model, consulting is simply concerned with the sort of management practice any decent, professional manager should possess. For example, the ability to diagnose problems or to develop interdiction or improvement strategies. At another, the key stages of the model emphasise influencing and sales skills. So that the ability to make a sale and develop a relatively generic, applicable managerial response to a perceived problem seem to be the pivotal skills possessed by the consultant. There must be an alternative explanation for the profession.

Of course, the self-referencing explanation of the consulting profession itself is that the practice is highly specialised and skilled, delivering a unique blend of high-valued competencies to businesses that do not keep those skills in-house. In other words, management consultants are specialist business "doctors," essential to the health of corporations and governments. Naturally enough, this explanation has driven recent trends within the profession that we have witnessed over the last quarter of a century or so. These can be analysed into two distinct drivers; one on the supply side and one on the demand.[2] For the former, as we have discussed in the preceding pages, the need for consulting businesses to seize market share and to diversify services has led to a full range of consultancy products from high-level corporate strategy to detailed sub-system practices such as e-commerce, technological development and implementation.

On the demand side, clients are witnessing this diversification and segmenting of the consulting market and using it to strengthen their own hands by running competitions between consulting providers and increasingly using market dynamics to hold consultants to account. A number of high-profile legal cases are testament to this trend. For example, at the turn of the century a client of Towers Perrin in the United States was suing the firm on the premise that generic analysis was being promoted by the client as unique insight. Clients have become more litigious to the extent that internal assurance is now the key focus of consultancy managing partners.[3] Within the United Kingdom there are examples of the Health Ministry and Home Office not paying consultants for major computer system implementations and software upgrades, so that market dynamics are increasingly used to moderate consultancy sales and delivery practices. Though, of course, the initial requirement for the employment of consultants in the first place seems not to be conceptualised or assessed.

This chapter has described and discussed what may be seen as alternative explanations of the practices of management consultancy. A commercial, highly rational justification of the subject, prefaced by the case that consultancy is the confluence of common sense and smart salesmanship. Perhaps, though, the explanations reside together, that the phenomenon of management consultancy can exist in both states.

For example, researchers in quantum physics address themselves to something that they call the "central mystery" of science.[4] This, perhaps, can best be described in the summary form of an idealised experiment. Imagine a source of electrons, an electric gun, if you like, similar to the tube to be found in a typical television set. Add to this a simple screen with two subatomic sized holes in it, and an electron detector. Electrons are then fired through these two holes and the results captured by scientists. Physicists report that what is observed is very strange.[5] Whenever an electron is detected by a researcher it behaves like a particle, but whenever the scientist is not physically monitoring the experiment, at that moment the electron behaves like, and possesses the physicality of a wave. It seems to exist concurrently in both states, as physical matter and energy wave. This is remarkable and difficult to explain using science's conventional analytical tools and constructs.

Likewise, the practices of management consultancy could be said to exist in a duality, as both a rational, legitimate discourse and change management dialectic, justifying and guiding perceived critical organisational change, but also at a deeper level as a force which exercises modes of power through the promotion of an omnipotent managerial solution to every problem, however complicated or fragile. Within this explanation management consultancy homogenises organisational responses to tensions and risks, which makes for an incredibly powerful and all-pervading management phenomenon.

Moreover, acceptance by clients within companies or project teams of the consultancy managerial agenda represents the absorption of a restraining, corralling, controlling power construct. These could be revealed by sociologists as an interlocking, complex, interdependent multiplicity of functions, behaviours, beliefs and mechanisms that generate individual and group meaning and understanding, aligning agency to this dominant narrative of management consultancy.

A narrative, however, that is superficially benign, rational and expressed in the causal, linear terms of the management transformation model which, once deployed, will yield economic efficiencies and greater management effectiveness. It can hardly be otherwise, for management consultancy measures the effects of these things through its own discourse and on its own terms. And when all is said, what could be more normal, desirable or altruistic than the quest to capture and import good management?

So management consultancy resides and can be explained in both states, that of the rational, of the common sense, and that of the powerful omnipotent discourse. The person within the client organisation, and consultants themselves, must exist and operate in these multilayered assemblages of purpose and purposefulness, enwrapped in what could be described as a social and managerial capillary of unified and unitary belief.

For many analysts and practitioners, consultancy is the application of common sense. This may be right, but it also seems to be so much more—a phenomenon with multiple, competing explanations and understandings. It makes the case for professional governance, oversight and regulation an important consideration that we shall come onto shortly.

Notes

1. See, for example, Mick Cope, *The Seven Cs of Consulting* (London: Prentice Hall, 2000).
2. Sugata Biswas and Daryl Twitchell, *Management Consulting: A Complete Guide to the Industry* (New York: John Wiley and Sons, 2002) pp. 24-28.
3. Author private research interview with consultancy leaders and stakeholders.
4. See J. Gribbin, *In Search of Superstrings* (Cambridge: Icon, 2007).
5. See L. Krauss, *Hiding in the Mirror* (New York: Viking, 2005).

9. Consultancy as Dependency—The Demand for Management Consultancy

Why Pay for Consultancy

If consultancy, in part, is the supposed judicious application of common sense, why is the global market as large as it is? Moreover, why do smart and intelligent businessmen and women, politicians and officials keep giving their shareholders and taxpayers' money to those who practise consultancy? In short, what is it about the relationship between a client (whether existing, new or, as yet, not even identified for a potential sale) and a consultant that is so compelling and, for the management consultant, profitable?

In this chapter we consider this relationship as a series of dependencies between those who pay and those who advise. The first point to make, of course, is to acknowledge that human motivations and actions are complex and highly nuanced. Consequently, I can only explore this subject in generalities and through the prism of my own experiences as I do not claim to know all, if any, of the secrets or ambitions of my erstwhile clients. Rather, I brigade my thoughts around the ideas of it potentially being exciting to contract consultants; activity displacing organisation progress; the false-promise of success and the allure of networks in an attempt to explain the durability of the relationship between client and consultant.

Being the Client Is Exciting

Being the client and having a number of bright, responsive people reporting to you and seeking to please you can be remarkably seductive, especially when there is none of the burdensome responsibilities of personnel management, employment law and rights and career development or management getting in the way. The simple view, therefore, is that people like to employ consultants because they get something back from the relationship as well as the subject of the engagement.

Without exception, in every engagement I have been involved with, the client's representative or project manager delighted in having a team of consultants jumping to his or her tune, reflecting back the disquiet he or she felt with their own organisation. With the UK Ministry of Defence, one of my clients, a senior female civil servant, would require the consulting team and personal staff to assemble in a meeting room ahead of her grand arrival. We were not permitted coffee or water ahead of the meeting, but the civil servant would arrive in tight-fitting sportswear carrying a large cup of coffee and a memo pad containing her thoughts of the moment. It thrilled her enormously to be holding dominion over expensive, suited consultants from the private sector, never missing an opportunity to, paradoxically, demonstrate both her superiority to the client team but also her total intellectual dependence upon it. The relationship was not a successful one though it taught all involved with it that many clients found the thrill of simply being a client remarkably invigorating.

In a similar vein, I had a client who was the project manager of a large, multi-site shopping centre whose principal operations were based in the UK and Australia. This man was charged by his company with building a large retail park to the west of the centre of London. He was a competent and confident professional of many years standing in his trade, but found the employment of consultants quite simply intoxicating. Whenever a team and I arrived on site we were greeted by the most extraordinary array of people detailed to meet us to escort us to the project manager's office. During the course of the engagement it became clear that pretty much everybody from the business on site had been scheduled to meet with us as though some kind of consulting magic dust would be blown onto the staff, impregnating them with mystical power of business analysis and insight. Either that or, as the consultants deduced, the project manager was on some kind of perverse ego trip, disrupting the everyday activities of his project to demonstrate that he could employ and manage consultants, somehow enhancing his status as a project manager.

If this sense of client excitement was present in both the public sector and construction business it was also to be found in sectors such as oil and gas. I would travel and send consulting teams to European and African cities and sites on the ad hoc whim or ill-formed impulse of a project manager from one of the global oil and gas businesses. Quite often they would pay our large fees and provide first-class travel merely to have us undertake or mentor risk and opportunity reviews, work that could easily have been performed within the business. But these men—always men—wanted to show that they could engage and control consultants almost as dancing puppets, demonstrating that they were powerful and important managers. The problem for me, even at the time when I was benefiting from these practices, was that the money being spent belonged to somebody, the shareholder or the taxpayer, and buying consultants almost "off-the-shelf" did not always represent good value for money or an effective, even considered, use of scarce resources.

Activity Displaces Progress

Having spoken to a number of past clients it is clear to me that the very act of employing a consulting team to address a particular requirement is invariably exciting for the client, reaffirming her or his sense of power and control. But it also has to be remembered that consultants are asked into a client's organisation supposedly to address a specific problem or set of concerns. The very activity of employing consultants can demonstrate to a client's stakeholders—the media, market analysts, shareholders, customers or, perhaps, even employees—that he or she is overtly working on the problem or concern. The act of conscious activity demonstrates that the client is attempting to manage and problem solve thereby, perhaps, buying valuable time to a struggling organisation. Consultants, though, are typically expensive and this activity can displace actual progress.

For example, I was asked to develop a Benefits Realisation Plan for a scientific research organisation. A Benefits Realisation Plan is a document that tracks inputs through an organisation's processes to its outputs and, thereafter, the outcomes engendered or benefits realised. Simply put, this organisation wanted to employ me because the organisation could not demonstrate to its funders what it was delivering in return for the large sums of money bestowed upon it. My engagement would take about six months to conclude at which time I would present my findings to the funding councils and private individuals who funded this business.

It became clear to me fairly early on that by consulting with me the board was not buying necessarily a solution, but what it really required from me was the breathing space to allow management to think through just how the organisation could reform and reshape itself. The act of employing a consultant on a six month review would buy them this time. In fact my conclusions and recommendations did not even feature in the change programme developed after six months to generate the necessary organisational transformation, though my consulting house was requested to run the programme. My purpose, cynical, expensive, though very understandable, was not to generate answers but to stall for time.

I suppose some might argue that this is a reasonable and tactical use of external expertise and a smart response if the organisation was able to transform and recover, securing its forward funding as a consequence. It could be conceded that this is so, but quite often I have experienced being deployed to a client site simply because the client had no idea how to deliver his programme or develop an appropriate organisational solution. The programme became the employment of a consulting team, and the consulting activity became the purpose for the organisation rather than an ingredient contributing to success.

A very sensitive defence programme was established to provide physical protection from a range of hazards and threats. I was sold out from my company as the programme lead providing advice and support to this team. There was little if any sense of how this programme could deliver the required outcomes of a successfully protected community so the schedules or Gantt charts, risk reviews and benefits planning *became* the programme. Activities relating to this laudable ambition of physically protecting a group of people became the project activities of the consultant so that little was achieved other than myriad performance reviews or risk analyses. But this still cost millions of dollars, with any benefits simply not understood let alone realised. Activity had displaced progress or the development of real, physical solutions. Looking back this was an accidental collusion between the consultant and the client; we had to do something, after all!

The False-promise of Success

Success in business or government service is a social rather than empirical phenomenon. If two parties to a problem believe that it has been solved and articulate this belief to others, the problem has been solved—at least "narratively." This is especially relevant, and powerful, in the context of management consultancy where "key performance indicators," the engagement "outputs" and "critical success factors" are developed and articulated by the consultant and sold to the client as part of the engagement solution. Consequently, success can be defined by the consultant and client without reference to evidence or data, which can be remarkably useful. Clients are making a financial investment, remember, when they engage with consultants. These same clients have stakeholders and superiors who will judge them on the quality and care of the investments made. It is in the client's interest to ensure that the consultant is successful, buying into the narrative of success. A failure, after all, is a failure in judgement of the client engaging with the consultant in the first place.

Consultants, naturally enough, are keen to diversify across a broad range of sectors as they offer their particular promise of success to ever more client groupings. This practice of diversification can build additional intellectual capital within the consulting organisation whilst simultaneously growing profits by helping the firm to capture a larger proportion of the consulting market. This quest for growth and profit maximisation is probably at the heart of a number of distinct trends I have been witness to over the years.

First, firms increasingly seek to merge or partner on bids with other businesses, usually in a quest to enhance existing competencies or reach. Second, firms have become much more internationalised emulating the largest consulting businesses, as they seek a broader geographical spread to reach more and more clients. Part of this trend is associated with the globalisation of the client base allowing synergies and efficiencies to flow between corporate clients and consultants. Third, information technology really has proven to be significantly transformational, so that information management systems, governance, strategy and change management are subjects best explored by a single consulting practice specialising in—simply everything. The promise of success is, somehow, legitimised and assured through this practice of globalised consulting.

The Allure of Networks

There is a significant cross-pollination between the client community and management consultancies. By this I mean that consultants recruit from their client organisations thereby gaining industry knowledge and clients recruit their consultants to embed management skills and personable, engaging personalities within their organisations. Developing networks to open up future employment opportunities is, consequently, an integral part of the relationship between client and consultant offering mutual benefits. Quite often, this is described as the "revolving door" between the advisory and client communities.

There are a number of factors worth exploring. It is not an exaggeration to say that market forces shape relationships. If a current client, or a member of his or her team, is alive to the possibility of working in consultancy sometime in the future they tend to be sympathetic to and supportive of the consultants they employ. A critical perspective can be replaced by an instinct to empathise and an acceptance of the insights and solutions offered by the consultant. Likewise, a consultant who is minded to move into commerce or industry can demonstrate his or her empathy with the targeted organisation sometimes at the expense of a proper and reflective critique. It is human nature, and I have witnessed it in some form on every engagement I have been privy to. Moreover, people corralled into soft networks via the revolving door have a shared view of the world that is reinforcing and legitimising the extensive use of consultants to undertake a variety of functions. In this way, for example, a recent trend has been for consultancies to practise as outsourcing agencies rather than change management specialists. Entire functions such as human resource management, finance or information technology can be outsourced to the consultancies who will, for a fee and long-term contract, expertly "deliver" the function that was traditionally contained by the client organisation in-house. The faith of the business to entrust such key functions to a consultancy has been developed in part by this network of relationships between client and consultant. In my own time as a consultant I have even advised on the development of the business case and investment appraisal that would demonstrate that the consulting solution was superior to the in-house alternative (that had probably been working satisfactorily for years). This could not have been achieved unless the client was predisposed to accepting the professional and functional superiority of the consulting solution.

These networks linking client and consultant often take the shape of professional bodies, such as accountancy or marketing institutes, universities (especially their business schools) and think tanks. Anywhere where the practices of consultancy can be explored, rationalised and legitimised through analysis and explanation can see informal networks prosper. If you like, there appears to be a dominant discourse of explanation validating the practices of consultancy.

This sense of dominant discourse sits within a long-standing critical tradition,[1] in that the narratives within society, manifested within the structures and processes that frame our lives, socialise and train our beliefs, behaviours and responses. This, in turn, represents a profound manifestation of power, both of society and of the self within society. Consequently, the networks of consultant and client have little choice but to be ensnared within the narrative they promote. This power is real and effective in shaping behaviours through a number of indirect and hidden ways which are most effective in securing compliance when these factors are least susceptible to observation. This inability to observe the hidden mechanisms of power and control in action inhibits us all within society and commerce. The mechanisms of power contained within the client-consultant relationship, consequently, both repress opposing behaviours and produce subjects socialised into society's beliefs, norms and practices.

As Marcuse observed,[2] these exercises and practices, along with the presence of common, enduring, systemic values, provide a universal discourse populated by a multiplicity of pervasive, self-validating hypotheses. As these combined narratives form a monopoly of knowledge, understanding and truth, the hypotheses themselves become "hypnotic definitions"[3] excluding any possibility of articulated dissent.

Psychologically, this is important to understanding the relationship between the client and the consultant enshrined within their networks. For they are established and accepted, and perhaps even further analysed, classified and embedded within scientific, managerial and organisational practices and explanations. Thus, one set of truths and realities prevents the generation of another, for the genealogy of understanding and meaning chooses one route of explanation at the expense of others.

Sociologically, the "problematisation" of an operation or an institution provides the dividing line between organisational best-practice, so-called, or failure, and between personal normality and deviancy. The authorities who define phenomena as problematic do so through their understanding of knowledge as applied through the self, imbued with positional authority and power. It is an intoxicating, self-referencing exposition of derived truth and understanding, through which non-conformity, even creativity, is repressed and rejected.

Much of the language of explanation and transformation is expressed in terms of project management. Indeed, the Association of Project Management (APM) actively talks of a managerial "body of knowledge" which is presented as both objectively fashioned and scientifically derived, unifying both client and consultant in a notion of best practice. The APM body of knowledge is subdivided into fifty-five knowledge areas embracing planning and control techniques, financial and management accounting technologies, risk management and even ecological environmental management. Project managers themselves have become acknowledged as global professionals, with authority as subject-matter experts, accredited with membership of international management institutes. The consultant and client have become "networked" in the objectivisation of these truths which become compelling and unavoidable.

A Complicated Relationship

There is, therefore, a sense that the relationship between the client and the consultant is complicated, mutually reinforcing and interdependent. It is, though, this sense of dependency that makes the management consulting profession so powerful and influential, warranting a consideration of how best to monitor and regulate the activity as a global profession. It is this question that we now turn to in the next short section below. The sheer scale of the consulting phenomenon, the size of the market and its omnipotence within the professional domain makes this one of the leading questions of governance and assurance that we face today in a globalised and interdependent world.

It is not a question, however, with an easy answer as regulation brings bureaucracy, and bureaucracy can represent an unwarranted and unwanted intrusion into the business relationship between client and consultant. Moreover, the dynamism of commerce is not easily regulated, despite what we tell ourselves, and regulation of government activities is fraught with tensions and false promises. We may just have to be content with doing our best, reaching for our higher values. Maybe we should ask a management consultant to help us with this?

Notes

1. Steven Lukes, *Power: A Radical View* (London: Macmillan, 2005).
2. H. Marcuse, *One Dimensional Man: Studies in the Ideology of Advanced Industrial Society* (London: Routledge and Kegan Paul, 1964).
3. Ibid., p. 56.

SECTION FOUR

10. Consultancy as Profession—The Need for Chartered Status and International Standards

Which Brings Us to Today

Today, there are hundreds of thousands of people employed or operating as management consultants globally. The engagement model followed, whilst bespoke to each company or practice, has a number of common features and factors as discussed in the preceding pages. But on volume, utility, value and sheer endurance the world sees, and should see, consultancy as a profession and a rich one at that. It is, of course, why so many young men and women from the leading business schools and universities join global and niche consulting businesses every year.

Of course, the status of "profession" and "professional" brings responsibilities. This chapter discusses just what those responsibilities should be, and how the acceptance and management of professional status should drive the organisation and conceptualisation of the management consulting profession. As we should expect when bright people come together, management consultancy has not been idle in embracing this agenda. The internationally recognised Certified Management Consultant (CMC) professional designation is being seen now more and more across the profession. Likewise, the Management Consulting Excellence (MCE) certification is in existence, but there is no corresponding professional institute, backed by statute, or international confederation, governing the profession or assuring its quality.

Yet, in specialist services, such as engineering or accountancy for example, the profession is regulated and governed by a standing body of subject-matter experts and their staff charged with maintaining and enhancing the long-term standing and reputation of the profession. These professional bodies often have chartered status within the countries in which they operate, which means that the profession has an exclusive grant of rights to the subject by the head of state or legislature detailing the profession's roles, responsibilities and obligations. Consequently, a member of the profession—a chartered accountant to take but one example—is a member of that professional body and can practise lawfully, having passed its many examinations and successfully operated in practice under the tutelage of the profession itself.

Let us consider this further. The Chartered Institute of Management Accountants is an international accountancy professional body specialising in management accounting, cost control and corporate strategic accounting. It is a highly credible and respected international body with many of its members occupying senior posts in government, commerce and industry. I happen to have been a chartered management accountant since 1999, having passed sixteen three-hour examinations over the preceding four years and demonstrated my competence in practice before serving as a management accountant in the UK with the Royal Air Force.

In contrast, to act as a management consultant, I required no validation, did not need to pass any Institution's exams or other tests and certainly did not enjoy chartered status or the professional, critical review of my peers or more experienced members of the management consulting profession. This seems very strange, especially as my range of responsibilities and engagements with business and government as a consultant were significantly greater than my professional contribution during my time as an accountant. Surely it must be possible for society to ensure that the consulting profession is regulated and governed in a similar fashion, perhaps even benefiting from chartered status on a par with the accountancy or engineering professions?

Having regulated chartered management consultants would allow those holding office to oversee both access to the profession through a range of application processes and examinations, and to ensure that members remained up to date and useful through the introduction and management of a profession development process. This needs to be neither bureaucratic nor organisationally onerous. An institution's professional development policy is, typically, an output based scheme focused on lifelong professional learning activities for members. The aim is the maintenance of a professional's work competency and standards within her or his current role, and the preparation of people for future roles within the profession. Members of the professional institute would be encouraged to maintain their own records to demonstrate compliance with the aim of continual professional development, with a random sample of members selected on a regular basis by the institute as a way of monitoring and assuring the quality of the scheme. This works well for the accountancy and legal professions in economies and societies around the world. It makes sense for management consultancy, as a professional practice, to be governed in the same manner.

Continual Professional Development

A continual professional development stance within a regulated national or international institute would allow the management consultancy profession to enshrine a quality assurance and improvement culture across the profession, embedding these goals into everyday practice. This would be remarkably beneficial for both client and practitioner alike, as the former would be offered professional guarantees of service associated with a regulated profession, whilst practitioners would be backed by a training and development regime tailored for their specific needs. It must be possible for the consulting profession to embrace such a reform, perhaps even benefiting from the sort of chartered status afforded to, for example, the accountancy, engineering and medical professions.

Take the Chartered Institute of Management Accountants (CIMA), an international accounting institute specialising in cost and management accounting. I am a member of CIMA, and to qualify I had to pass sixteen three-hour examinations over a four year training period and demonstrate effectiveness in practice. The Institute's professionalism is built upon six key and unambiguous development stages, as follows:

- The definition of current and desired future roles and the specific needs of today's and tomorrow's clients or employers;
- Assessing the development needs and goals to identify knowledge or skills gaps against identified capabilities and competencies;
- Designing development and professional training activities to meet the necessary learning objectives;
- Acting upon these identified needs;
- Reflecting upon and assessing the impact of each activity and intervention to ensure that the learning objective has been met, and
- Continually evaluating the professional record and planning activities for the years ahead as a continual, auditable, professional practice—critically, validated and assured by the Institute.

The formalisation of professional development in this manner would have enormous benefits for the management consulting profession. Practitioners would continually upgrade and update their skills and competencies, act in a reflective and thoughtful manner to develop the consulting body of knowledge beyond the sales competencies that have continually peppered this analysis. Moreover, clients would access the profession knowing that a clear, auditable and learned methodology existed to match their business requirements to the diagnostic and process solutions available to the management consultant. Such is the stuff of a proper, modern professional body, ready to take its place in a highly complicated and fast-changing internationalised economy and globalised community. The discipline of management consultancy, and those who operate beneath its banner, together must heed the call.

11. Concluding Thoughts

This book makes a clear and unambiguous argument that we should take care and be clear-eyed and focused when engaging with the management consultancy profession. As such, it is a treatise rather than an exhaustive history or piece of unbiased research. In consequence, the pages drip with subjective opinion and personal perspective as well as the artefacts of research. Nonetheless, I have tried to be fair and personally reflective in the sense that, for me, management consultancy exists in multiple states and through a variety of explanations. This is not far from the stances that many social theorists would adopt today nor indeed from our smart, everyday instinct that there is more than one way to look at a subject or fellow human being.

It has been a privilege to write this book, to think about an amorphous profession that is profoundly and increasingly significant both nationally and internationally, and to unpack my own experiences of working as a consultant. My contention is a simple one: the world is remarkably complicated and uncertain whilst the phenomenon of management consultancy quite often suggests that it can be dissected and diagnosed, and successful consulting engagements implemented through common "change models." Whilst this plays well as both a case of business development and engagement practice, inevitably through the ever-present PowerPoint pack, it can become less convincing when long-term benefits are captured and assessed.

Management consultancy, of course, is here to stay, representing a powerful set of practices and a strong lobbying voice, influencing both business and government. Indeed, there is much utility to be derived from an ethical, informed and knowledgeable "outsider" testing a client organisation and recommending necessary improvements or changes. As a consequence, this practice needs to be treated as an important profession and appropriately regulated—self-regulation may, actually, be fine (and certainly a step in the right direction)—in the same manner as we would expect with other important societal professions such as accountancy, medicine or the law.

In talking to a number of senior business leaders and consultants it is clear that the influence of management consultancy, especially through its major global firms, is now seen as an omnipresent feature of the global business ecosystem. As well as conducting change initiatives and offering specialist services such as risk management and strategy development, the large advisory businesses will couple long-term outsourcing service delivery with initial consulting diagnoses. This means that these businesses will extensively partner with governments and large corporations for the long run, generating a level of mutual dependency we may not have witnessed before within our globalised economy. If this is right, the urgency with which management consultancy as a profession is regulated and governed becomes a pressing, and prescient, debate for today.

When I practised as a consultant it became all too clear that making a sale was the most highly valued skill a consultant could possess. I was uncomfortable with this at the time and I am far from enamoured with it now. An uncertain and highly complicated world needs an ethical and regulated consulting profession beyond the salesmanship that was my experience. To be fair, many consulting companies embrace this thought themselves, and internal assurance and quality control increasingly exercises the leadership of consulting businesses and partnerships. My hope is that this book helps contribute to this most important of debates, now, whilst we have time to ponder the power and importance of this phenomenon.

Further Reading

To explore the many managerial, governmental, societal, commercial, social, defence and security issues touched-upon by this work, the following additional reading is suggested:

Armstrong, M. and T. Stephens. (2005). *Management and Leadership*. London: Kogan Page.

Bachrach, P. and M. Baratz. (1970). *Power and Poverty: Theory and Practice*. New York: Oxford University Press.

Ball, A. (1983). *Modern Politics and Government*. London: Macmillan.

Bauman, Z. (1989). *Legislators and Interpreters: On Modernity, Post-modernity and Intellectuals*. New York: Free Association Books.

Beck, U. (1988). "On the way to the industrial risk society? Outline of an Argument," *Thesis Eleven*, 23, pp. 86-103.

Beck, U. (1992). *Risk Society: Towards a New Modernity*. (Trans. by Mark Ritter) London: Sage.

Bell, U. (2000). *Sierra Leone: Building on a Hard-Won Peace*. UN Chronicle Issue 4.

Best, S. and D. Kellner. (1997). *The Postmodern Turn*. New York: The Guildford Press.

Boden, R., P. Gummett, D. Cox and K. Barker. (1998). "Men in White Coats ... men in Grey Suits," *Accounting, Auditing and Accountability Journal*, vol. 11, no. 3, pp. 267-91.

Bottomore, T. (1979). *Political Sociology*. London: Hutchinson.

Bourdieu, P. (1990). *The Logic of Practice*, trans. Richard Nice. Stanford: Stanford University Press.

Bourdieu, P. (2000). *Pascalian Meditations*. Trans. by Richard Nice. Stanford: Stanford University Press.

Burke, R. (2003). *Project Management*. London: Wiley

Cameron, K. and R. Quinn. (1999). *Diagnosing and Changing Organisational Culture*. Stanford: Addison-Wesley.

Chia, R. (2004). *Foundations of Management Knowledge: Assumptions and Limitations*. Paper No. 01/04, University of Exeter.

Child, S. (1964). *British Management Thought*. London: Allen & Unwin.

Contractor, F. and P. Lorange. (1988). *Co-operative Strategies in International Business: Joint Ventures and Technology Partnerships between Firms.* Lexington: Lexington Books.

Cope, M. (2000). *The Seven Cs of Consulting.* London: Prentice Hall.

Coulson, A. (2008). "Value for Money in PFI Proposals," *Public Administration* 86.2, pp. 438-98.

Daft, R. (1995). *Organization: Theory and Design.* New York: West.

Dahl, R. (1957). "The Concept of Power," *Behavioural Science*, 2: pp. 201-15, reprinted in Scott (ed.) 1994.

Dahl, R. (1961). *Who Governs? Democracy and Power in an American City.* New Haven: Yale University Press.

Dahl, R. (1976). *Modern Political Analysis.* Englewood Cliffs: Prentice Hall.

Day, R. (2005). "Clearing up Implicit Knowledge," in *Journal of the American Society for Information Science and Technology*, vol. 56.6, pp. 630-35.

Dean, M. (1999). "Normalizing Democracy: Foucault and Habermas on law, liberalism and democracy," in Ashenden, S. and D. Owen (eds.), *Foucault contra Habermas.* London: Sage.

Dean, M. (2003) [1997]. "Sociology after Society," in D. Owen (ed.). *Sociology after Postmodernism.* London: Sage.

Dean, M. (2007). *Governmentality—Power and Rule in Modern Society.* Los Angeles: Sage Publications.

Denzin, N. (1994). *Symbolic Interactionism and Cultural Studies.* Oxford: Blackwell.

Dodgson, A. (1991). *The Management of Technological Collaboration.* SPRU, UK.

Dodgson, A. (1991). "Technological Collaboration and Organisational Learning: A Preliminary View of Some Key Issues," *DRC Discussion Paper.* Sussex, UK.

Donzelot, J. (1979). *The Policing of Families.* New York: Pantheon.

Donzelot, J. (1984). *Social Invention.* Paris: Fayard.

DPA (2003). The Defence Procurement Agency, Ministry of Defence. *Annual Report 2003.* London: HMSO.

Drucker, P. (1955). *The Landmark of Tomorrow.* London: Sage.

Drucker, P. (1977). *People and Performance.* London: Heinemann.

Drury, C. (2001). *Management Accounting for Business Decisions.* London: Thomson.

Du Gay, P. (2000). *In Praise of Bureaucracy.* London: Sage.

Dunleavy, P. and C. Hood. (1994). "From old public administration to new public management," *Public Money and Management*, vol. 14, no. 3 pp. 9-16.

Easton, D. (1957). *The Political System: an Inquiry into the State of Political Science.* Cambridge: CUP.

Easton, D. (1965). *A Framework for Political Analysis.* Cambridge: CUP.

Eatwell, J. (1982). *Whatever Happened to Britain?* London: BBC.

Edwards, P. and J. Shaoul. (2003). "Partnerships: For Better, for Worse?" in

Accounting, Auditing and Accountability Journal, vol. 1.6, no. 3, pp. 397-421.
Edward, P., J. Shaoul, A. Stafford and L. Arblaster. (2004). *Evaluating the Operation of PFI in Roads and Hospitals.* London: ACCA.
Eulau, H. (1963). *Journeys in Politics.* London: Tavistock.

Fayol, H. (1949). *General and Industrial Management.* London: Pitman.
Falk, R. (1999). *Human Rights Horizons: The Pursuit of Justice in a Globalizing World.* London: Blackwell.
Foucault, M. (1969). *The Order of Things: An Archaeology of the Human Sciences.* London: Tavistock.
Foucault, M. (1975). *Discipline and Punish: The Birth of the Prison.* New York: Random House.
Foucault, M. (1980). *Power/Knowledge: Selected Interviews and other Writings 1972-1977.* Brighton: Harvester.
Foucault, M. (1982). "The Subject and Power," in H. Dreyfus and P. Rabinow, *Michel Foucault: Beyond Structuralism and Hermeneutics.* Chicago: Chicago University Press.
Foucault, M. (1988). "Politics and Reason" in L. Kritzman (ed.). *Politics, Philosophy, Culture: Interviews and other Writings.* New York: Routledge.
Foucault, M. (1991). "Governmentality," in G. Burchell, C. Gordon and P. Miller (eds.). *The Foucault Effect: Studies in Governmentality.* London: Harvester Wheatsheaf.
Foucault, M. (1994). "Critical Theory/Intellectual History" in M. Kelly (ed.). *Critique and Power: Recasting the Foucault/Habermas Debate.* Cambridge, MA: MIT Press
Franklin, P. (2006). "Explication as a Philosophical Exercise," in T. Gibson (ed.). *Organisations and People,* vol. 13.3, pp. 6-11.
Fraser, N. (1989). *Unruly Practices: Gender and Discourses in Contemporary Critical Theory.* Cambridge: Polity Press.
Friedman, M. (1980). *Free to Choose: A Personal Statement.* London: Pelican.
Friedman, M. (2000). *Capitalism and Freedom.* London: Routledge.
Froud, J. (2003). "The Private Finance Initiative—Risk, Uncertainty and the State," *Accounting, Organisations and Society,* 28(6) pp. 567-89.

Gaffney, D. and A. Pollock. (1999). "Pump Priming the PFI." *Public Money and Management,* vol. 17.3, pp. 11-16.
Gershon, P. (2004) [1999]. *Review of Civil Procurement in Central Government.* London: HM Treasury.
Giddens, A. (1990). *The Consequences of Modernity.* Cambridge: Polity Press.
Giddens, A. (1991). *Modernity and Self-Identity.* Cambridge: Polity Press.
GODP (1971). *Government Organisation for Defence Procurement and Civil Aerospace.*
Goodwin, B. (1982). *Using Political Ideas.* Chichester: John Wiley & Sons.

Gribbin, J. (2007). *In Search of Superstrings*. Cambridge: Icon.

Haddon-Cave, C. (2009). *The Nimrod Review. An Independent Review into the broader issues surrounding the loss of RAF Nimrod MR2 XV230 in Afghanistan in 2006*. London: The Stationery Office.

Hague, R. and M. Harrop. (1982). *Comparative Government: An Introduction*. London: Macmillan.

Handy, C. (2004). *The New Alchemists*. London: Hutchinson.

Haralambas, M. (1980). *Sociology: Themes and Perspectives*. Oxford: OUP.

Hayek, F. (1944). *Pure Theory of Capital*. Oxford: Blackwell.

Hayek, F. (1979). *Law, Legislation and Liberty, vol. 3. The Political Order of a Free People*. London: Routledge & Kegan Paul.

Hindess, B. (1996). *Discourses of Power: From Hobbes to Foucault*. Oxford: Blackwell.

Hindess, B. (1997). "Politics and Governmentality," *Economy and Society* 26(2), pp. 257-72.

Hindess, B. (1998). "Divide and Rule: the International Character of Modern Citizenship," *European Journal of Social Theory* 1(1), pp. 57-70.

Hirst, P. (1981). "The Genesis of the Social," *Politics and Power* 3, pp. 67-82.

Hirst, P. (1993). *Associative Democracy: New Forms of Economic and Social Governance*. Cambridge: Polity Press

Hood, C. (1990). "De-Sir Humphreyfying the Westminster Model of Bureaucracy: A New Style of Governance?" *Governance*, vol. 3, no. 2 pp. 205-14.

Hopwood, A. and P. Miller. (1994). *Accounting as Social and Institutional Practice*. Cambridge: CUP.

House of Commons (HOC) (1982). House of Commons. Public Accounts Committee Annual Report.

House of Commons (HOC) (1998). House of Commons. Defence Committee Eighth Report. London: The Stationery Office.

House of Commons (HOC) (2004a). House of Commons. Public Accounts Committee. *MoD Major Projects Report 2004*. London: The Stationery Office.

House of Commons (HOC) (2004b). House of Commons. Public Accounts Committee Annual Report.

House of Commons (HOC) (2008). House of Commons. Public Accounts Committee. *MoD Major Projects Report 2008*. London: The Stationery Office.

IISS (2008). The International Institute of Strategic Studies. *The Military Balance*. London: Routledge.

Kincaid, B. (1999). *Dancing with the Dinosaur*. Oxford: Alden.

Kincaid, B. (2002). *Dinosaur in Permafrost*. Oxford: Alden.

Koch, R. (2000). *Strategy*. London: Prentice Hall.

Kotter, J. (1996). *Organisations and Leadership*. London: Collins.

Lamming, R. (1993). *Beyond Partnership*. London: Prentice Hall.

The Labour Party (1995). *Strategy for a Secure Future.* London: The Labour Party.

Larner, W. (2000). "Neoliberalism: Policy, Ideology, Governmentality," *Studies in Political Economy (63).* University of Auckland.

Lee, S. (1982). *Aspects of European History.* London: Methuen.

Lemke, T. (2000). *Foucault, Governmentality und Critique.* Amherst: MA.

Lonsdale, C. (2005). "Post-contractual lock-in and the UK Private Finance Initiative (PFI)," *Public Administration* 83 (1), pp. 67-88.

Lukes, S. (1974). "Relativism Cognitive and Moral," Supplementary Proceedings of the Aristotelian Society," *Essays in Social Theory.* London: Macmillan.

Lukes, S. (2005). *Power, A Radical View.* London: Macmillan.

Marcuse, H. (1964). *One-Dimensional Man: Studies in the Ideology of Advanced Industrial Society.* London: Routledge & Kegan Paul.

McKinsey. (1991). *Strength to Innovate.* London: McKinsey & Co.

McKinsey. (2003). *Efficiency and Effectiveness: A Guide.* London: McKinsey & Co.

Miles, R. and C. Snow. (1986). *Organizational Strategy, Structure and Process.* New York: McGraw-Hill.

Mill, J. S. (1989) [1869]. On the Subjection of Women in JS Mill, *On Liberty and Other Writings,* S. Collini (ed). Cambridge: CUP.

Miller, P and T. O'Leary. (1993). "Accounting expertise and the politics of the product: economic citizenship and modes of corporate governance," *Accounting, Organisations and Society* 18(2/3). pp. 187-206.

Minson, J. (1993). *Questions of Conduct: Sexual Harassment, Citizenship and Government.* London: Macmillan.

Mintzberg, H. (1973). "Strategy Making in Three Modes," *California Management Review* 16.2, pp. 44-53.

MoD (1987). Ministry of Defence. *Learning from Experience. A Report on the Arrangements for Managing Major Projects in the MODPE.*

MoD (1997). Ministry of Defence. *British Defence Doctrine.* Joint Warfare Publication 0-01. London: MoD CS(M)G.

MoD (1998). Ministry of Defence. *The Strategic Defence Review (SDR).* London: The Stationery Office.

MoD (2002). Ministry of Defence. *The Smart Acquisition Handbook Edition 4.* London: MoD.

MoD (2003). Ministry of Defence. *Annual Report and Accounts.* London: The Stationery Office.

MoD (2004). Ministry of Defence. *The Smart Acquisition Handbook Edition 5.* London: MoD.

MoD (2005). Ministry of Defence. *Annual Report and Accounts.* London: The Stationery Office.

MoD (2008). Ministry of Defence. *Blueprint: The Future Operating Model for DE&S.*

MoD (2009). Ministry of Defence. *Review of Acquisition: An Independent Report by Bernard Gray.*

Mowery, D. (1988). *International Collaborative Ventures in US Manufacturing.* Cambridge, MA: Ballinger.

Nadel, S. (1957). *The Intellectual in Contemporary Capitalist Society.* Cambridge: CUP.

NAO (1995). The National Audit Office. *Procurement in the Ministry of Defence.* London: The Stationery Office.

NAO (1998). National Audit Office. C&AG's Report. *MoD Major Projects Report.* London: The Stationery Office.

NAO (1999). National Audit Office. C&AG's Report. *MoD Major Projects Report.* London: The Stationery Office.

NAO (2000). The National Audit Office. *Supporting Innovation: Managing Risks in Government Departments.* London: The Stationery Office.

NAO (2003). National Audit Office. C&AG's Report. *MoD Major Projects Report.* London: The Stationery Office.

NAO (2004). National Audit Office. C&AG's Report. *MoD Major Projects Report.* London: The Stationery Office.

NAO (2005). National Audit Office. C&AG's Report. *MoD Major Projects Report.* London: The Stationery Office.

NAO (2006). National Audit Office. C&AG's Report. *MoD Major Projects Report.* London: The Stationery Office.

NAO (2007). National Audit Office. C&AG's Report. *MoD Major Projects Report.* London: The Stationery Office.

OMS (1961). Office of the Minister for Science. *Report on the Committee on the Management and Control of Research and Development.*

Oughton, J. (1998). *The UK Defence Review.* London: The Stationery Office.

Osborne, D. and T. Gaebler. (1993). *Reinventing Government: How the Entrepreneurial Spirit is Transforming the Public Sector.* New York: Plume Books.

Page, L. (2006). *Lions, Donkeys and Dinosaurs.* London: William Heinemann.

Parsons, T. (1937). *The Structure of Social Action.* New York: McGraw-Hill.

Parsons, T. (1953). *The Social System.* New York: The Free Press.

Parsons, T. (1960). *Structure and Process in Modern Societies.* Chicago: The Free Press.

Pedler, M., T. Boydell and J. Burgoyne. (1986). *A Manager's Guide to Self-development.* Maidenhead: McGraw-Hill.

PMI (1996), Project Management Institute. *A Guide to the Project Management Body of Knowledge.* London: PMI Publication.

Pollock, G. (2002). *Museums after Modernism.* Blackwell: Oxford.

Polsby, N. (1963). *Community Power and Political Theory.* New Haven CT: Yale University Press.

Prahalad, C. and G. Hamel. (1990). "The Core Competencies of the Corporation," *Harvard Business Review,* May-June.

Rabinow, P. (1997). *Essays on the Anthropology of Reason*. Princeton USA.
Rothwell, R. (1981). *Industrial Innovation and Public Policy*. London: Frances Pinter.
Rose, N. (1985). *The Psychological Complex: Politics, Psychology and Society in England 1869-1939*. London: Routledge & Kegan Paul.
Rose, N. (1989). *Governing the Soul—The Shaping of the Private Self*. London: Routledge.
Rose, N. (1999). *Powers of Liberty*. Cambridge: CUP.
Russell, B. (1946). *History of Western Philosophy*. London: George Allen & Unwin.

Schattschneider, E. (1960). *The Semi-Sovereign People: A Realist's View of Democracy in America*. New York: Holt, Rheinhart and Winston.
Senge, P. (1990). *The Fifth Discipline*. London: Random House.
Senge, P. (1994). *The Fifth Discipline Fieldbook*. London: Random House.
Shaoul, J. (1995). *NHS Trusts: A Capital Way of Operating*. London: ACCA.
Shaoul, J. (2005). *The Regulation of and Accountability for New Forms of Public Procurement*. Working Paper Series.
Simon, H. (1960). *Administrative Behaviour*. London: Macmillan.
Steger, M. (1998). *Globalism: the new market ideology*. Oxford: OUP.
Steger, M. (2003). *Globalization*. Oxford: OUP.
Stewart, R. (1982). *Choices for the Manager*. New Jersey: Prentice Hall.

Taylor, F. (1911). *The Principles of Scientific Management*. New York: Harper.
Teece, D. (1986). "Profiting from Technological Innovation: Implications for integration, collaboration, licensing and public policy," *Research Policy*, vol. 15, pp. 285-305.
Tomlinson, C. (1999). *The Differentiated Classroom*. London: Collins.
Treary, M. and F. Wiersema. (1996). *The Discipline of Market-Leaders*. Washington DC: Perseus.
Tully, J. (1993). "Governing Conduct," *An Approach to Political Philosophy: Locke in Contexts*. Cambridge: CUP.

Webb, S. and B. Webb. (1935). *English Local Government*. London: Macmillan.
Weber, M. (1958). *The Protestant Ethic and the Spirit of Capitalism*. New York: Charles Scribner's.
Willis, P. (1977). *Learning to labour*. Westmead: Saxon House.

Yeatman, A. (1994). *Postmodern Revisionings of the Political*. New York: Routledge.
Yeatman, A. (1998). "Interpreting Contemporary Contractualism," in M. Dean and B. Hindess (eds.). *Governing Australia: Studies in Contemporary Rationalities of Government*. Melbourne: CUP. Pp. 227-41.
Young, I. (1990). *Justice and Politics of Difference*. Princeton: PUP.

Zaleznik, D. (2004). *Executive's Guide to Understanding People*. New York: Palgrave Macmillan.